What Your Counselor Never Told You

Books by Dr. Backus

Finding the Freedom of Self-Control

The Good News About Worry

The Healing Power of a Christian Mind

The Hidden Rift With God

Learning to Tell Myself the Truth

Teaching Your Children to Tell Themselves the Truth
    (with Candace Backus)

Telling Each Other the Truth

Telling the Truth to Troubled People

Telling Yourself the Truth (with Marie Chapian)

What Your Counselor Never Told You

What Your Counselor Never Told You

SEVEN SECRETS REVEALED
Conquer the Power of
Sin in Your Life

DR. WILLIAM BACKUS

Author of *Telling Yourself the Truth*

BETHANYHOUSE

MINNEAPOLIS, MINNESOTA

Published by Bethany House Publishers
11400 Hampshire Avenue South
Bloomington, Minnesota 55438

Bethany House Publishers is a division of
Baker Publishing Group, Grand Rapids, Michigan.

Printed in the United States of America

Library of Congress Cataloging-in-Publication Data

Backus, William D.
    What your counselor never told you : seven secrets revealed—conquer the power of sin in your life / by William Backus.
       p.   cm.
    ISBN 0-7642-2392-5
    1. Deadly sins. 2. Sin—Psychology. 3. Psychotherapy—Religious aspects—Christianity. I. Title.
    BV4626 .B33 2000
    241'.3—dc21
                                         00-011425

To Thomas J. Kiresuk, Ph.D.:

Director, NIH-funded Center for Addiction and
Alternative Medicine Research
Minneapolis Medical Research Foundation;
Chief Clinical Psychologist
Hennepin County Medical Center;
Professor of Clinical Psychology
University of Minnesota Medical School;
Director, Program Evaluation Resource Center
Minneapolis Medical Research Foundation

His lifelong fascination with the Seven Deadly Sins as
psychological traits sparked my interest; his knowledge
and research skills undergirded my work; without his
generous gifts of time and teaching, this book never
would have been written.

WILLIAM BACKUS is founder of the Center for Christian Psychological Services, and an ordained clergyman in the Lutheran church. He is also a licensed Consulting Psychologist. He has a master's degree in theology from Concordia Seminary in St. Louis and a Ph.D. in clinical psychology from the University of Minnesota. Dr. Backus has conducted follow-up studies of his clients, which show a 95 percent improvement rate, compared to a 67 percent success rate for other methods of therapy. The difference, Dr. Backus says, is "the truth of God as revealed in the Word."

Acknowledgments

It is my pleasure to acknowledge the valuable assistance of all those who contributed to the development of the Sin Test and to this book about sin and psychopathology.

Thanks are due especially to:

Tom Kiresuk, Ph.D., to whom this book is dedicated, and who helped me in more ways than I can possibly enumerate;

The Wheat Ridge Foundation, whose material support enabled this research;

The Reverend Edward May, Executive Director of the Wheat Ridge Foundation at the time this research was done;

All those students, staff, and patients who willingly served as test subjects;

Milton Rudnick, Th.D., who when the going got rough supplied solace and located numerous student volunteers;

Paul Mauger, Ph.D., Zigrids Stelmachers, Ph.D., and Seymour Gross, Ph.D., for their assistance and encouragement;

Paul Meehl, Ph.D., who taught me trait theory;

Robert Sherman, Ph.D., who supplied statistical consultation and assistance;

Christopher Soderstrom, the editor who worked hard to improve things while supplying enormous amounts of reinforcement along the way;

Gary and Carol Johnson and the many employees at Bethany House Publishers who are so skilled at the care and feeding of authors.

Contents

What Happened to the Seven Deadly Sins?

Seven deadly sins of old the Good Life tried to fix,
Freud stood surety for Lust, then there were six;
Six deadly sins danced a brisk satanic jive,
Strachey* banished Gluttony, then there were five;
Five deadly sins pursued their soul-seducing war,
Covetousness? Good for business. Then there were four;
Four deadly sins bestrode the world with devilish glee,
Envy—whom? There's no one left. Then there were three;
Three deadly sins planned what evil they could do,
Sloth? It's lack of vitamins. Then there were two;
Two deadly sins enjoyed a spot of fiendish fun,
The dollar loan abolished Pride, then there was one;
One deadly sin—by Beelzebub! the last,
Anger's simply gland secretion, Sinner—danger's past!
Autres temps, Autres moeurs ("Other times, other morals")

—Stanley J. Sharpless
The New Statesman and Nation
July 5, 1947

---

*Strachey, (Giles) Lytton (1880–1932). A British historian and biographer noted for his urbane, witty, critical (and worldly) biographical works, including *Eminent Victorians* (1918).

Introduction

Sick or Sinful?

Sandy* consulted me for treatment of her painful feelings. "I don't love my husband. I can't stand living with him any longer! I feel terribly depressed. I think I'm going to have some kind of breakdown. Can you help me? I'm so upset."

"Sandy, can you tell me what's troubling you?" I asked.

"I really need something for my depression. I'm so stressed I can hardly function, especially at home. But I don't want a full-blown psychoanalysis," she added.

She was clearly feeling disturbed, but she also seemed functional. I asked her to go back to the beginning, to recount the history of her distressing situation.

"Do we really have to go into the past? I feel terrible *now*."

"I understand, and I know it's difficult for you to do this. But I want to help, and I need to learn all about your relationship with your husband if I am to be of assistance to you."

Reluctantly she reviewed the story of her marriage, making it obvious that she was in a hurry to get to the point: She wanted

---

*The stories of individual cases have been altered. Names and all identifying details have been changed for the protection of real people. If you think you recognize someone, the resemblance is purely coincidental.

out. It was so awful she couldn't bear it for another day. She'd done her part, but the results she desired hadn't come and she was ready to call it quits.

Sometimes patients want their therapist to give them permission to do things they aren't sure are right. Was this Sandy's goal? Was I supposed to help her pull the plug and make the break? Would she skip over the positive aspects of the history so that I would tell her what she wanted to hear? I knew that wouldn't be a good idea; instead, I resolved to listen without prejudice. To do so, I needed to slow her down, to encourage her to share details that would shed light on the big picture.

I learned that Sandy and Jason had been high-school sweethearts. She had noticed the boy with the bluest eyes she had ever seen on the first day of her French class, junior year. Did he notice her? She thought he might; most boys did. And more than a few kept noticing; Jason was one of them. When after class the next day he came up beside her as they walked to the lunchroom, she felt a little thrill in the pit of her stomach.

"Didn't I see you at the church I visited last Sunday?" he asked. "Up toward the front on the right side?"

"Maybe, but I didn't see *you*. You must have left early."

"Yeah, I had to go before the benediction. I wanted to visit my grandma in the hospital, and I had to catch a ride. She's really sick. The doc says she may not pull through. I love her so much."

It seemed to Sandy that she had never talked to a boy with such a compassionate heart, such a compelling voice. *Where has he been?* she wondered. He seemed to be more caring than the other boys she had known. She thought about him a long time that day, and she could hardly wait until third period the next morning. She decided they would get to know each other better.

(As Sandy rehearsed all this for me, her expression changed as memories of the time when the flame of love burned brightly came back, and she recaptured momentarily some of the old feelings. Depression? That had been her initial complaint. I kept listening, almost certain that Sandy's difficulty was something else.)

"Hey!" he hailed her.

"Hey!" she tried to sound casual, tried not to let him see how strongly he attracted her.

"I'm Jason—Jason Stabler."

"My name is Sandy Sorenson," she replied, happy but not surprised that this model specimen of youth should be interested in her. She really was smitten with Jason. His looks were striking, but what she liked most were his winning charm, his vibrant personality, and his affectionate tenderness. As their relationship grew stronger, she felt that Jason was a boy who would put her needs first, ahead of his own. Even her mom thought he was a dream come true. And she didn't worry about it when her dad complained about his being somewhat lazy, having little ambition, and not showing much interest in what he would do with his life after they graduated in two years. That was just Daddy—he was always a bit critical of the guys she brought home. She was sure Jason had a bright future, and she liked the idea of being alongside him in it. She was certain he would do whatever it took to please her.

So they fell in love and were married shortly after graduation. Both too immature to marry, they believed firmly that their love would conquer all. Two years later a baby girl was born. But now Sandy began to notice a trickle of worry floating on the margin of her stream of thought, way out on the edge. Gradually, her concerns multiplied. They were short of money, sometimes to the point where rent payments had to wait. Why had she and Jason not even considered how they would make it on Jason's near-poverty-line income? She imagined she'd just taken for granted that he would step out of school into a fine career. But he didn't seem to mind being a retail clerk in a big discount store. Sandy had assumed that Jason would display the same restless ambition to advance that she had seen in her father. Now it appeared that Jason would never be capable of supporting a woman with Sandy's ideals about the good life. They had planned for her to stay home and give all her attention to the children, but they had also expected that Jason would be promoted rapidly into the upper echelons of company management. It hadn't happened, and as they fell further and further behind, Sandy decided she had to get a job.

"Sandy, honey, it will only be for a short time—until we get 'caught up.' Meantime, I bet your Mom would love to watch Katie while you're at work. I'll be getting a raise soon—it's over-due," Jason promised, assuring her of his love. But as it turned out, expected raises came less often than they had hoped, and there was no way the Stablers could get along on Jason's income alone. They argued more—and more and more—mostly about finances.

"I didn't like it when I had to get a job, when Jase wouldn't even consider looking for something that paid more. It made me mad that he cared more for being comfortable than he cared for Katie and me. I told him if he really loved us he'd take care of us, but he blew up and yelled at me that I should get off his back, that he was doing all he could," Sandy shared. "I began to realize that Daddy was right. Jason had never grown up. I had fallen for a cute boy who was still just that—a boy. I used to think he was charming. Now I can't stand him!"

Twelve years ago she had married the man of her dreams. Now she was convinced he was intolerable.

I listened carefully to her story, especially in view of her re-luctance to talk about it. Sandy repeatedly said she was de-pressed, but I kept thinking—and feeling—that I was picking up something else. Hers was not the deflated ego, the heavy, drag-ging movements, the tired, drawn features that so often signal serious depressive maladies. Yet I also realized that patients oc-casionally cover up their symptoms, especially in milder cases of mood disorder.

I made the usual inquiries about the vegetative symptoms of depression. She had a diminished appetite and had lost a little weight over the past two months. But her sleep was not dis-turbed, except for being awakened by Jason's snoring. What a racket! She hated sleeping with him. How had she ever come to think she loved him? Most nights she would finally move to the living room sofa, where she managed to fall asleep for a few hours.

"How long have you been so angry and so miserable?" I asked. I didn't use the word "depressed" because Sandy showed none of the large-scale signs of depression, such as self-devaluation, sleep and/or appetite difficulties, listlessness, inactivity. What she did show was irritation, frustration, and anger.

"For a while, I guess. I'm sick of life being this way."

Chronic feelings of anger, because they are very unpleasant, are often labeled *depression* by clients. Sometimes such clients believe they are depressed rather than angry because, they think, depression is an illness they suffer from, while anger sounds like something with moral connotations, an implication they may resist. Therefore, I decided to proceed gently. I chose the neutral label "bad feelings" for now.

"So you would like to get over your bad feelings and work out your problems with Jason?" I asked her. I was quite aware that she had not said precisely that. I wanted to hear what Paul Harvey calls "the *rest* of the story."

"Well . . ." she hesitated.

"Well, what?" She hadn't yet come to the crux of the problem. I had heard only chapter one.

"It's hard to tell you about this part. I think I feel guilty. There's someone else. He isn't a bit like Jason. He's older, he wants to start his own database service company, and he understands exactly how I feel. We met at work. One day we had lunch together and started to talk. Before I knew it I was pouring out my heart to him. It was such a relief. And he was so considerate, so thoughtful. You see, it turned out he needed someone to talk to also, and his wife doesn't understand him either."

"Does he have any children?"

"No. That's one of the problems in his marriage. She doesn't want to be tied down. She wants to pursue her career and thinks it wouldn't be fair to have children and have someone else taking care of them."

"So you're having an affair! How is that solving any of your difficulties with Jason's lack of ambition or your lover's wife's preference for a personal career?"

"We are *not* having an affair. We love each other, but we

aren't sleeping together. We have agreed that it would be wrong for us to have sex before we—"

"Before you what?"

"Before we get married. We don't think that would be fair to our spouses, and besides, we're Christians and we know it would be wrong in God's eyes. We know we have to wait. For now, all we do is talk. But for some reason I still feel guilty. This whole thing has made me so depressed. I do need your help. Can you give me some medication? Can you help me get over this? I just can't handle this depression by myself anymore."

"It must be a terrible feeling to realize you are married to a man you don't love," I replied. And I meant it. What an awful valley of the shadow for this young woman, especially when she had once felt nothing but idealistic delight in and love for her husband! To think that now her dream had come crashing down and shattered to bits. Sandy began to cry.

I waited and then went on. "I'm not going to ask you to take an antidepressant, and I can't give you a formula to make the bad feelings go away this minute. I need to see you again in a week. We can go over your test results, and maybe, if you still want my help, we can work out a plan for handling this thing."

I didn't want to tell her yet that she was feeling bad because she was angry and vengeful and not because she was sick. Our relationship was far too fragile and her expectations far too unrealistic for that. And I did want to check her test results to see if they indicated that she would cope with the truth, for the truth alone would set her free. But I was not at all certain she would be willing to take the only road that could possibly lead her to freedom.

Sandy had, probably unconsciously, gone to great lengths to evade the truth. She'd hidden from herself a number of things, including, probably, her love for Jason, as well as the fact that she was furious at his unwillingness to do what *she* wanted. She had told herself she was depressed, and she'd hoped that a psychologist would understand, make her feel better, and be open and accepting of her wish to end her present marriage and pursue a "better" one. After all, the man she now idealized seemed so unlike Jason (and, though she didn't realize it was a huge factor, very much like her own father).

Sandy had also hoped I would help her overlook the moral truth that she had duties in her marriage and that she was sinning in what was already an adulterous relationship—even if she was not sleeping with her lover. I wondered, too, if she was even slightly aware of her angry desire to punish Jason by being "in love" with someone else. On the issue of maturity, she had no grounds to find fault with her husband.

She agreed to return in a week, and she did. I learned that she had been raised to believe that whatever she wanted must be right as long as she couldn't see how it could hurt her. She had also been taught that life was supposed to be positive, upbeat, and pleasant. If she had feelings to the contrary, she was suffering from an illness, and the best bet for getting over that would be to see a counselor and/or take some medication. Now she was suffering considerable pain because of stress—the stress she was causing herself by telling herself it was not right that she should encounter financial difficulties in her marriage or that Jason should oppose her wishes, especially when she was (to herself) so obviously right. On the contrary, what could be more just and righteous than to admit that she had made a mistake in marrying too young? To her it seemed perfectly reasonable that another man would appeal to her—one who, unlike Jason, would be interested only in her and in meeting her needs.

Sandy's test results did not support her diagnosis of depression any more than her symptoms had. Like many others today, she was miserable, not depressed. She was miserable because she was sinning and using one of the most common cover-ups available in our society. I was not interested in "getting rid of" her guilt. Guilt is not a "weird feeling" but a healthy and appropriate reaction of the conscience given to us by our Creator.

Yet would I be able to convince Sandy that her problem was sin, not sickness? So many people would expect a psychologist, especially a Christian psychologist, to accept her misery as evidence of emotional illness and to leave the domain of the moral and spiritual, of right and wrong, to her pastor. But I also knew that sometimes, maybe very often, those who come to see psychologists are functioning quite well, and the fact that they present miserable feelings only means their psychic equipment is operating as it was intended to. It's *supposed* to hurt when you are telling yourself untruths and acting accordingly! It's *supposed* to feel bad when you sin. And this woman was sinning against her *God* and His plan for her life, against her *daughter*, who would never grow up the same if she had to be raised by her mom and a man who was not her father, and against her *husband*, who, while imperfect, was joined to her before both God and man. She needed to find the tremendous moral courage and spiritual energy to reverse course, to go back and make a new start with the man she'd promised to stick with for better or worse "till death parts us."

What I Am *Not* Saying and What I *Am* Saying

My training in the Graduate School of Psychology at the University of Minnesota, my reading in professional journals, and my hearing of learned papers at psychology conferences (even sometimes pastoral conferences) had taught me the accepted answer: Psychologists deal with illness, not sin; psychology is a science, and science does not make value judgments; people like Sandy—people suffering, sometimes in deep anguish, sometimes claiming they can't control their behavior—must be sick, and it is the psychologist's duty to either heal them or refer them to someone who does not make moral judgments. And I have to admit that even though I agree with M. Scott Peck that what we are confronting in some cases is evil—and with Karl Menninger's plaintive title question, "Whatever Became of Sin?"—I still find it difficult to tell a troubled client whose pain is very real that it is my opinion that an underlying cause is sin and that the treatment is repentance and faith in Jesus Christ.

Nevertheless, I also know that in spite of the fact that psychotherapy, properly done, has been demonstrated by empirical research to be effective—not once but over and over again—

there still are many instances where therapy has failed. The best psychotropic medication (drugs that act on the mind) is effective in the majority of correctly diagnosed patients, but what about the roughly one-third for whom it is not helpful? Could one of the reasons be that not everyone who has emotional difficulties has an emotional illness? If the skin on your back begins to feel sore when you are lying in the summer sun, you would be wise not to diagnose the problem as "sick skin" but to get out of the sunshine. Long before anybody thought of anxiety neuroses or major depressive episodes, people knew that something deep inside them hurt when they did something immoral and that the real cure had to be capable of making things right with God, other people, and themselves, or else it was no cure at all. It is certain that some people who come for counseling, even some of those who believe they are ill, would be better diagnosed as sinful.

I have to admit something else to you: I am terrified that what I am saying may be misunderstood. So let me tell you what I do not intend to say. First, I am *not* saying that all the emotional and behavioral problems we human beings encounter are simply sins by other names. We are all sinners, but not everything that goes wrong is a direct consequence of our own choices. People do victimize and hurt other people, and circumstances we can do nothing about may inflict suffering. Many clients are clearly sick, having a real illness with an etiology (cause or origin), an underlying pathology (something abnormal or diseased), a course (the expected path the illness will take if it isn't treated adequately), and sometimes, an effective treatment. Examples of these are people suffering from brain injury, schizophrenia, or bipolar disorder. They are sinners as all humans are, but what is making them unhappy and causing them to behave in seemingly senseless ways is a malfunctioning nervous system.

Second, I am *not* saying that every problem we encounter in the clinic is *either* sickness *or* sin. Some of our clients are suffering from painful current circumstances. Others present a complex interaction of sin and illness, like the depressed person who gets drunk regularly to try to make the depression go away. Any true clinical depression, to the best of our current knowledge, involves disordered neurochemistry, even if the depression is brought on or maintained by sinful behavior. Neither Christian lay counselors nor professional therapists should shoehorn everybody into their favorite compartment.

Third, I *am* saying that a fair number of problem situations that clients bring to us are related to their own sinful actions, habits, and attitudes. I am arguing and trying to demonstrate in this book that sin *may be* the pertinent issue and that where it is, repentance and faith in the redeeming work of Christ Jesus constitute the proper cure. As you read *What Your Counselor Never Told You*, you may conclude that what distresses you (or if you are a counselor, some of your clients) these days does not involve sin. But you might be surprised. You might agree that at least for some, sin is an important alternative diagnosis. In fact, you may develop insight into your own depravity and so discover an even more powerful key to the door of wholeness than psychology knows or provides. This conclusion might appeal to you because *there is a God-given remedy for sin*, without which nobody is ever fully healed of the human condition of alienation. That remedy is Jesus Christ. That He is an effective cure is the primary advantage of making sure our diagnoses do not overlook sin. This is true whether you are a curious person wanting to resolve personal problems, move ahead in holiness, or be set free from a sinful complex; or whether you are a clinical counselor seeking a more complete understanding of psychopathology and its relation to sin.

Psychology and psychiatry have powerful engines responsible for pulling heavy loads, but these engines are often propelled by secularist reductionism.* To some extent both trains (psychology and psychiatry) have derailed and may be running off the tracks toward inevitable disaster. At least as represented by

---

*"Secularism" concedes relevance only to the worldly and temporal. "Reductionism" is a paradigm or way of thinking that reduces complex data or phenomena to oversimplified terms and concepts. In this case, it is the world's way of seeing "reality" that eliminates the possibility of spiritual/eternal origin.

their official organizations and their academic fountainheads, they regard secularist beliefs and values as axiomatic (taken for granted, or self-evident). Secular thought offers no real cure for the pain and unhappiness that afflicts the human heart in this culture. Having left the railway of truth, it has lost the ability to distinguish good from evil, virtue from vice, truth from falsehood.

Because persons who need a real cure for their broken hearts seek it from psychologists and psychiatrists, they need an adequate diagnosis and prognosis. Abandoning the awareness of sin and goodness, of evil and God, has a sad consequence. Helpers become helpless when confronting those who are not merely depressives, hysterics, hypochondriacs, and obsessives who need to be made more like the other inhabitants of the world, but rather sinners in need of healing and salvation.

I am now ready to tell you more about Sandy. When she returned, I said, "I need to tell you something—and I hope it will be something you can accept because it is the truth."

"I want you to tell me the truth. It's all I've ever wanted to hear," she replied.

She listened carefully to me and to the feedback we got from her psychological testing. There was no evidence of depression. However, we established that Sandy was angry—angry and guilty. She was also described as impulsive, one who sometimes made decisions in haste, without enough forethought.

Sandy gradually realized that her "understanding" lover had not showed much discernment for her real needs, concern for Jason, or compassion for his own wife. In fact, she came to realize that she was using him to inflict punishment on Jason. She was bitter and resentful, so she would hurt Jason for not doing as she'd planned. She assumed that others should meet her every need and that her part of the contract was to make them accept her and her wishes "as is." She saw her sinful selfishness, turned to God for forgiveness, asked for strength to commit herself to righteousness, confessed to Jason, and asked him to join her in working things out. Jason didn't change his employment, but he did agree to request a significant raise—which his boss gave him, along with apologies for not having done so sooner.

Although anger was an appropriate diagnosis for Sandy, there is a difficulty for professional therapists here: The *DSM-IV*, the diagnostic manual of mental illnesses, does not provide for such a diagnosis. However, like Sandy, many clients *need* to confront problems related to anger, for it underlies much misery.

The History of the Seven Deadly Sins

There was a time when the diagnoses of human problems were made by clergy. For centuries, then, people learned to consider the possibility that their own sins lay at the root of their difficulties. Therefore, a list of sins might in those earlier centuries have constituted a sort of "diagnostic manual." One such list, the Seven Deadly Sins, is fairly well known in popular culture. About thirty years ago Dudley Moore and Raquel Welch starred in a film entitled *Bedazzled*, a comic version of Goethe's *Faust* in which seven actors played the personified Seven Deadly Sins. Somewhat more recently, Brad Pitt and Morgan Freeman starred in the detective thriller *Seven*, in which a series of murders were committed by a fanatic who wanted to punish those whom he believed were egregious examples of the seven sins.

But the Seven Deadly Sins system was not devised for entertainment—far from it. It was created as a moral/spiritual diagnostic aid to persons who were totally serious about their Christian lives. A diagnostic system is what the Seven Deadly Sins arrangement has been for centuries—long before the current secular clinical diagnostic scheme was ever conceived. *Pride, Envy, Anger, Greed, Sloth, Lust,* and *Gluttony* were considered extremely potent causes of human misery, while insight into one's own sinfulness was viewed as a constructive step toward wholeness. Some history and background might be in order.

Clinical psychologists and psychiatrists currently make diagnoses by referring to a book with the engaging title of *DSM-IV: Diagnostic and Statistical Manual of Mental Disorders, Fourth Edition.* A gigantic volume of 882 pages, it describes the disorders of the human mind. Since it was first published, subsequent editions have expanded exponentially—like Jack's beanstalk. The 1952 version, *DSM-II*, covered only 132 pages. Since then, more of the things people don't like about themselves and others have been given official status as "psychiatric disorders." *A lot more*. Some, though described in language sounding like descriptions of illnesses, could, in a spiritually based system, be called sins. Should they be? Is it valid to criticize a completely secular system as incomplete? Is it surprising to learn that the church once had such a diagnostic system—a spiritually based list of behavioral disorders used for diagnosing human problems?

Although some authors assert, as does theologian Randy Rowland in his recent book on the Seven Deadly Sins,[1] that this list originated with Pope Gregory the Great (deceased A.D. 604), the fact is that the sin list reaches back at least sixteen hundred years, and probably beyond. The length of the list did vary from time to time, as did the precise names of the sins included. Nonetheless, the listing of deadly sins or vices began long ago, in the earlier centuries of Christianity, when certain believers sought to deepen their spiritual lives and draw nearer to God by living alone in the barren wastes of the Egyptian desert with the scorpions and centipedes. These people endeavored to subdue their sinful desires in order that they might draw closer to the Lord; through prayer and obedience they sought lives guided only by the pure promptings of the Holy Spirit.

The catalog of deadly sins was in common use among these hermits. One of the leaders, Evagrius of Pontus (born A.D. 346), wrote about them; another, John Cassian (c. A.D. fourth and fifth centuries), left the wilderness and took the sin list with him to Ireland, where he founded monasteries and also wrote at length about the deadly sins. As the custom of private confession and absolution spread in the church, the sin list became a guide used by pastors/confessors for examination and for counseling penitents—a kind of diagnostic manual of sins. We might think of this early pastoral ministry as a form of spiritual therapy.

Over the ensuing centuries, pastoral use of this system led to the development of deep clinical insights into the nature of man. The Seven Deadly Sins caught the imagination of the Christian world. Many theologians, including St. Thomas Aquinas, Pope St. Gregory the Great, and the mystic St. John of the Cross, wrote about the Seven Deadly Sins. Nontheological writers who discussed the Seven Deadly Sins were top-of the-line authors like Dante, Chaucer, Gower, Langland, and others.

The understanding of these concepts has grown over the past sixteen or seventeen centuries with the contributions of many wise and discerning theologians and writers. I have tried to distill some of their perceptions for your use. Why? Partly because, as a practicing clinical psychologist working with diagnosis and treatment for the past thirty years, I have become convinced that the systems derived from secular science alone are good but inadequate. A scientific view of human behavior, constrained by the dogmas of secularism, must be incomplete, even distorted, because science has limited itself to consideration of *material* cause and effect. Since most sensible people know that humans have a moral and spiritual dimension, and that theological and philosophical issues make a huge difference in the way people think and act, it only makes sense to consider the spiritual disarray caused by human sinfulness when a doctor treats someone for a behavioral/emotional/mental disorder.

The Sin Test

I developed an inventory for researching the relationships between sin and psychological disorders. This instrument has no official name, but we can call it the *Sin Test*. Because the Seven Deadly Sins arrangement has such a long history and rich background, I used some of the writings of theologians and others about the Seven to construct a sin inventory. This tool has functioned as an examination for individuals that yields a profile of seven scores on the Seven Deadly Sins.

To test the instrument itself, I initially gave the Sin Test to four experimental groups: 70 summer school students at a

Christian college, consisting of in-service church workers and college students; 57 assorted psychologists, social workers, psychiatrists, nurses, students in various clinical fields, pharmacology, and medicine, and friends and spouses of these subjects; 101 inpatients on the psychiatry service of a large general hospital; and 40 outpatients receiving treatment for various psychological disorders in the clinic of a large general hospital.[2] All subjects were given MMPIs.[3] For the inpatient group, charts and psychiatric diagnoses were available.

I went looking for empirical evidence that might answer several questions: (1) Would a test work to measure sins and sinfulness? Could we collect meaningful data about sin and sinners with such a tool? (2) Do people in treatment for psychological disorders tend on the average to have higher total "sin scores" than those who are not in treatment? (3) Are specific sins related to specific psychiatric diagnoses? For example, do people who score high in sloth also score high on the MMPI depression scale? Do patients who have been diagnosed and/or described as depressed by their doctors score higher on the sloth scale than others? Are there other relationships between specific sins and specific diagnoses? All these questions were answered in the affirmative to my satisfaction.

One question remained (it will interest readers sophisticated in trait theory and test theory): (4) Do the various subtraits and dispositions declared by the theologians to belong together actually hold together statistically? Let me explain with an example: The theologians had written that slothful people are both sorrowful and relatively inactive. My question was, would items measuring *both* those two characteristics tend to be affirmed by people scoring high on sloth *more regularly* than they were affirmed by people scoring high on some other sins? If they did, it would mean that the theologians correctly discerned that the deadly sin of sloth was an actual trait having various dispositions—such as sorrow and inactivity—that varied in tandem. The answer to this fourth question, too, proved to be yes: Statistically derived "intercorrelations" confirmed the theologians. The sins *were* found as subtraits and dispositions in people, which enabled probabilistic predictions about expected behavior.

"The Seven Deadly Sins" seems to have been the most popular title for this arrangement of traits. I call the sins by this title because of its widespread usage, but, strictly speaking, it is not entirely accurate for several reasons. For one thing, some writers have worked with eight sins instead of seven. This was the case with John Cassian; the "extra" sin he called *Vainglory*.

Moreover, the sins are not "deadly" like cyanide in the sense that they immediately kill everyone who is guilty of them. The Seven Deadly Sins lead to death and damnation only for the unbelieving and impenitent sinner—the same as any other sin.

And finally, the Seven Deadly Sins arrangement has had different designations over the centuries. Cassian and others have called them the *Seven Vices*, some have called them the *Seven Capital Sins*, and still others have used the term *Seven Cardinal Sins*. The idea behind the latter two is that these sins are like the mouths of rivers from which flow many streams. We can use the term *traits* for the Deadly Sins themselves and *subtraits* or *lower-level dispositions* for the clusters of behaviors that come from them.

Notes

1. Randy Rowland, *The Sins We Love: Embracing Brokenness, Hoping for Wholeness* (New York: Doubleday, 2000).
2. A detailed report of the research, theories, procedures, and results may be purchased from University Microfilms, Inc., Ann Arbor, Michigan. Complete ordering information: Backus, Donald William (1926–) "The Seven Deadly Sins: Their Meaning and Measurement." University of Minnesota, Ph.D., 1969, Psychology, clinical. Copyright by Donald William Backus, 1969. No claims are made here or elsewhere that the validity of the Sin Test has been thoroughly demonstrated. It may be used as a suggestion for further self-examination.
3. *The Minnesota Multiphasic Personality Inventory*, a 566-item portfolio yielding a profile of scores on eleven clinical scales and numerous additional scales. Only the clinical scales were used in this research.

Chapter 1

Taking Sin Seriously

In the courtroom, the two brothers appeared so youthful, robust, and soft-spoken that most of the jury found it difficult not to melt with compassion. On trial in California, accused of blowing away the faces of their parents with shotguns, Lyle and Eric Menendez admitted freely that on August 20, 1989, they had ambushed their parents with deadly gunfire. But, they argued earnestly, the cause of their appalling behavior was to be found in a history of dreadful abuse at the cruel hands of Jose and Kitty Menendez, their father and mother—abuse so terrifying that at last the brothers were unable to save their own lives. As the members of the jury were shown ghastly photographs from the horrible crime scene, attorneys argued that the boys had been made ill with fear of what they believed to be their parents' supernatural power. Their defenders insisted that since they were rendered so psychologically vulnerable by abusive treatment, the law must consider them innocent scapegoats, desperate to save themselves and salvage something from life, bearing the scars inflicted by the evil of their parents-turned-victims.

The trial turned on the question we look at in this book:

Were Lyle (age twenty-seven) and Eric (age twenty-four) responsible for the grizzly double killing they readily acknowledged having committed? Or were they so warped by mistreatment and emotional bruising that they could not be held responsible for their terrible actions? Did they kill because they were sick or because they were sinful—or both?

On March 20, 1996, the Menendez brothers were convicted of first-degree murder. At this writing, they are both serving life prison terms without the possibility of parole. Lyle is held at the California Correctional Institution at Tehachapi; Eric is at the California State Prison in Sacramento County.

The search for "root causes" of tragic behavior—pop psychology—has nearly everywhere become a red-hot topic. Someone does something outrageous, and we ask, almost reflexively, "What caused *that?*" *That* can refer to a shocking mass shooting, a sudden and unexpected criminal act by a trusted public figure, or the discovery that a relative has become psychotic. You might even stumble upon disorder or instability (neurosis) in yourself and wonder, "What caused me to think or do *that?*"

The more we learn about behavior, the more the possible answers multiply. If you read about the causes of, say, alcoholism, crime, or neurosis, you may only find yourself more confused than ever. Is the cause genetic? Or is it cultural? Could it be family-related? Is it, as some psychologists insist, reinforcement (consequences that are rewarding)? Sometimes cause-seeking is employed to free an individual from blame and responsibility, as if finding a cause for a behavior requires us to forget that the perpetrator made a vile choice.

Psychologists have helped to create myths about the process of causing (causation). "Experts" inform us that murder is caused by the easy availability of guns, rape is caused by childhood conflicts, poverty is caused by bad public housing, compulsions are caused by harsh toilet training, and homosexuality is caused by genes, though there is little evidence that any of these are the real villains. Even if one of these factors were proven to be *a* cause of troublesome behavior, it would never stand alone. As Aristotle (384–322 B.C.) noted, an event has not only one but several causes.

Although there are other ways to imagine multiple causes, one of the first writers on causation, Aristotle, described four distinct types of cause: *material, formal, efficient,* and *final.*

Suppose someone prepares a gourmet dish using pork tenderloin. Aristotle would say that pork is the *material* cause of the dish; the dish's appearance and taste might be its *formal* cause; the effort and energy of the chef is the dish's *efficient* cause; and finally the chef's intended result is the delicacy's *final* cause.

Another way to divide up multiple causes of a phenomenon is to notice that most events have both *proximal* and *distal* causes. A *proximal* cause is the cause closest to the actual event, while a *distal* cause is one that occurs earlier in the chain of events. Imagine you and I are playing a game of pool. I hit the cue ball, which then hits the nine ball, which in turn knocks the eight ball into the pocket. The *proximal* cause of my losing the game would be the nine ball nudging the eight ball, while *distal* causes would be both the cue ball contacting the nine ball and my cue hitting the cue ball.

How true this is of human thoughts and actions! And when a behavior is disastrous, overlooking important causes is a mistake with catastrophic consequences. Finding a counselor who can help get to the "root of the problem" isn't a bad scenario, as far as it goes. But when all causes are assumed in advance to be secular—*worldly* or *temporal*—this approach can be woefully inadequate and misleading.

The most overlooked cause of all is *sin.*

Avoiding the Truth

Do you remember Henry, the easygoing, permissive colonel from the TV series *M*A*S*H* (the one everyone liked, except Frank, the rigid, authoritarian surgeon)? I once worked in a hospital where the chief psychiatrist reminded me of Henry; he knew his way around psychiatry but his sophistication in philosophy and theology would hardly survive comparison with that of a freshly confirmed eighth grader. Hospital rules required that I apply to him for permission when I wanted to administer the Sin Test to patients. His reply startled me.

"I don't believe in sin," he said, taking a stance unusually tough even for staff doctors who didn't care much for God. We negotiated a compromise: I could administer the exam for experimental purposes, but I must not call it a "Sin Test." "Values Inventory" would be acceptable.

Even if they believe in the reality of sin on Sundays, behavioral experts seem determined, *en masse*, not to notice sin in their practice of soul healing. In fact, many go to great lengths to disregard it altogether. Like the crazy aunt kept tucked away in the attic lest visitors discover the family's humiliating disgrace, the idea of sin often seems to be deliberately hidden from view.

Why? Because the core idea in secular philosophies is that science *must* explain everything without reference to a transcendent deity. Accordingly, the concept of *sin* must be ruled illegitimate, for the meaning of the word itself is grounded in the idea of God. Due to the dominant popular slant on psychological phenomena, doctor and patient, counselor and counselee, will probably presume that whatever the root cause is, it cannot be sin. Yet in spite of popular terminology, sin doesn't mean "problem"—it means *transgression against God's law*.

God's Word identifies the consequences of human sin as enormous, drastic, and awful, for they include death and all of life's miseries. "As sin came into the world through one man and death through sin, and so death spread to all men because all men sinned" (Romans 5:12). It's hard to think of any human wretchedness that is not traceable to sin. From God's perfect viewpoint, the underlying cause of human misfortune, of sickness and pain, of relationships crashing, and of the entire human enterprise ending in death, is human sinfulness. Sin is the indirect, distal cause of my emotional anguish, while my self-devaluative beliefs might be one of the more proximal causes. Of course, there are times (like those we are considering in this book) when sin is a direct, proximal cause of our disorders. With deeper understanding of the complexities of causation, we see that our psychological disorders can have a number of causes, even when sin lurks at the bottom of the problem.

"Good Taste" Counseling

Why is the role of sin in human behavioral disorders not taken seriously by therapists? Because in today's culture labeling somebody's actions as "sinful" is politically incorrect; "good taste" requires that we avoid such terminology. We assume that if we say, "Jones is a sick narcissist" or "Smith has an emotional illness brought on by childhood deprivation," we have made things clear without pointing a finger at the individual. Secular thought has replaced lists of sins with lists of illnesses. *Low self-esteem* has replaced *sinful pride*, *victimhood* has replaced *envy*, being *disadvantaged* has replaced being *greedy*, and so on.

As we examine ourselves in the light of certain *sin trait* descriptions, we will consider whether terms like *sickness* can really do justice to all that is radically wrong with our psyches. Would it not be closer to God's psychology to recognize that often the problem involves *sin*? If we approached our struggles with due attention to our sin traits, might we get better therapeutic results? Would it frequently be more truthful and therefore more liberating to diagnose specific *sins* in place of specific *neuroses*? (In other instances, it might be wise to consider the contributions of both sickness and sin.)

Do *Christian* Counselors Avoid "Sin Talk"?

A quick check of your nearest Christian bookseller's stock will turn up few volumes on this subject among the many works on counseling. Readers? Well, they too often prefer "success" stories; and sin, by definition, is not about success. Before you jump to the conclusion that I am planning to pin all psychological aches and pains on our misdeeds, allow me to explain.

Even while we consider God's wrathful reaction to human sin, we dare not overlook the paradox: He loves sinners and does whatever it takes to show mercy and compassion to us. We must

never think of God's burning wrath, inflamed by our wickedness, without at the same time envisioning Jesus' shepherding
care as He, in His own parable, climbs over rocky crags to scoop
up the lost sheep, the sinner, bringing her to a place of rescue.
God's wrath and God's grace must both be real to us. "You can't
have one without the other."

The truth is that *not everything that is wrong in life is a direct
result of sin.* Nor is every problem we encounter our own doing,
pure and simple. But it seems clear that *some* of them are, and if
we admit that most behavioral events have several causes, we
may see that those afflictions we *don't* actually bring upon ourselves can be aggravated by our sinful reactions. Yes, traumas
not of our own making can clobber us psychologically, and
heavy weights we didn't choose to bear may be strapped to our
shoulders, caused by other agents, heedless of our protests. But
we will often strike pay dirt if we ask not only "Who has done
wrong to me?" but also "What role does my own doing play in
my present misery?"

To ignore this second question is a terrible error. Take a look
at one more way to break down the idea of causation: There are
necessary causes and *sufficient* causes. A *necessary* cause is a
cause without which the caused event could not possibly happen. For instance, streptococcus bacterium is a *necessary* cause
of strep throat. It *can* cause strep throat, but it doesn't always do
so; at the same time, one cannot contract strep throat without it.
On the other hand, a *sufficient* cause is all it takes to produce a
particular result *regardless of other conditions.* A blood alcohol
level of .10 (or .08 in some states) is considered sufficient to
produce impaired driving, no matter what.

According to the Bible, *a considerable cause of most human
disorders is human sin.* Not the only cause but an important one;
not a *sufficient* cause but a *necessary* one. Sinfulness cannot be a
sufficient cause of shooting sprees by high school kids; after all,
everybody is a sinner, and only an infinitesimal few commit
murder. But sin is a *necessary* cause of such things, because
without a sinful nature people would never intentionally commit
murder. Were sin missing entirely, there would be no murder,

no rape, no child molestation, no drunkenness, and fewer people with disordered minds or disarrayed emotions. What is astounding is the human propensity for denying the reality of personal evil.

Why Study Sin?

We must examine sin because awareness is a big part of the cure, and for this ill there *is* a remedy. Contrary to many social and psychological problems, sin has a treatment that has been demonstrated to be effective. Unlike most suspects usually labeled *root causes*, such as growing up without a father or a mother, lack of parental affection, suffering parental abuse, and sexual victimization, *there is an antidote for sin*. In fact, the remediation (cure) of sin is the explicit purpose of the working of God the Father in history—of the incarnation, baptism, fasting, temptation, passion, agony, crucifixion, death, burial, resurrection, and ascension of Jesus Christ—and of the indwelling of the Holy Spirit in human hearts. The practice of regular daily *repentance* is our role in this sublime therapy.

During the course of my hospital-based investigation into the Seven Deadly Sins, I worked alongside ten or twelve other clinicians in a large room. One day Sister Catherine, a bright, lively little nun whose policy was to allow herself to look only at positive traits, asked what I was doing.

"I'm studying sin," I replied, probably too abruptly.

"Sin?!" she exploded. "Why?"

"I want to construct a sin test—a diagnostic instrument for error—so that people can discover what their most troublesome sin traits are."

Sister Catherine was flabbergasted. "Why don't you work on the *virtues*?" she snapped. "Sin is such a depressing subject!" Having settled the matter with finality, she never asked again about my research. Perhaps I ought to have told her more, for my purpose was not to wallow in sin but to discover whether sin and mental disorders were closely related or maybe even identical in some instances. I was hoping to provide help and hope for sinners who were being treated with nothing but secular philosophies. I have since learned that Sister Catherine was not alone in dismissing the subject as too dismal. Many of us, though we may not be quite as outspoken as she, want to escape having to think about our faults. We may even choose to avoid the concept of sin altogether.

Maybe we believe that our sins are minor, that we don't have many problems. Or perhaps we think, *"Jesus has paid for my sins, and I feel better when I concentrate on positive, comforting things. It does no good to look at my ugly side."* Is this the right perspective? Not entirely. We need to be honest about sin because in doing so we will be honest about ourselves. We're *all* sinners, and there's a good chance that some of our life problems are entwined with the issue of sin. Therefore, examining sin is a case of *need*, a requirement for health, if you will, like drinking water (cf., 1 Corinthians 11:28).

Think of it this way: Unless we are willing to look at sin, we won't be aware of its pervasive depth in our character. Without this awareness, we can't perceive our need for forgiveness. Without perceiving and acknowledging this need, Christ's atoning power will not be released in our lives. And without atoning power . . . we remain mired in bondage to sin.

We won't care much for God's forgiveness or become enthusiastic believers in it until we understand the dimension of our sin and its function in producing our needs, problems, hurts, and losses. Imagine if your friend said, "I forgive you for your bad treatment of me." Would you be glad to hear this if you hadn't the slightest idea what he was talking about, if from your point of view you'd treated him in an exemplary (or even acceptable) fashion? You'd need to learn from your friend what you'd done to harm him—diagnosis—and become convinced that your actions (or words, or absence of them) were damaging before you would be interested in his forgiveness. Grace can neither be understood nor desired without truthfulness—without things being acknowledged for what they are.

I am aiming to engage you in what might be seen as a series of personal diagnostic and treatment sessions. If these lead to repentance and faith and hearty cooperation with the Holy Spirit, the outcome will be a new dimension to your life in Christ. You will be able to see how sin disorders lurk beneath many—maybe most—psychological problems. When these maladies are recognized for what they are, the straightforward individual inventories in this book will be followed by change wherever change is needed.

Stains on God's Creation

Sin and sinfulness have marked and spoiled God's creation like an indelible stain penetrating a piece of clothing. Sin makes human existence difficult and unhappy, brings on sickness and death, undermines God's perfect plans for His world, and scars nature so that all creation groans and travails under the heavy load of human evil. Creation itself doesn't sin; plants, animals, weather, and so forth are under no moral law, rightly acting according to their nature. They are, however, victims of the sinful behavior of humanity; human nature worships its own instincts, a fact clearly exhibited in paganism, or nature religion.

William Golding's novel *Lord of the Flies* is a chilling tale about a group of English choirboys, angelic children, whose plane crashes near a remote and uninhabited island. No one comes to rescue them, and they are left to their own devices. The boys shape their own degenerate culture, making a chilling transition from the civilized, principled behavior of their upbringing to barbaric savagery. Telling the tale of their progressive return to moral and spiritual corruption, Golding shows us what we are seeing enacted in real life: the sinful, evil depths to which human nature, left without spiritual restraints, sinks. *Lord of the Flies* leaves us with a diagnosis, but no remedy.

It is not that we haven't looked for a way out. We've tried political systems—monarchies, oligarchies, dictatorships, republics, democracies. We've tried economic systems from capitalism to socialism to amalgamations involving measures of various means for controlling behavior. We've advanced medicine and surgery for overcoming sickness and death. We've invented and built devices for saving labor and increasing private and public wealth. We've trained for psychological and psychiatric interventions intended to alter human actions and motivations. But none of our efforts has ever proved effective in eliminating the power of sin.

I am not trying to say that none of them has been *helpful* in checking some undesirable behaviors and their painful consequences. But there are few specific treatments, let alone *cures*, for these evils, and *none* devised by man has been able to eradicate sin. I once heard a behavioral geneticist at the University of Minnesota declare that, given the power to engineer human breeding, he was confident that he and his colleagues would be able to rid humankind of sin. But is science really the answer?

How Tough It Is to Be Good!

"I'm so frustrated. I want to please God. I try to be good—really, I try hard, especially since I've been coming in to see you." Glenn, like a growing number of men in my case load, had become hooked on pornography. Like so many, he had discovered that what seemed to him at the outset to be no more than a peccadillo—a sneak peek at some tantalizing Internet pages—had swiftly become a high-strength habit. He was discovering the truth about sin and its power to enslave a human being.

The snares of porn addiction! This trap is harder to break out of than most people can imagine. But it isn't really so different from the snares of other sins; for instance, intemperate and irrational anger, chronic attention-grabbing, endless efforts to fill spiritual holes with money and its promises, or slurping too many gooey chocolate sundaes. You probably know about some of this from your own bitter experience. Perhaps you are reading this book because you want to learn more about the subtle seductions of habitual sinful attitudes and actions with a view toward getting free.

God's Remedy

God alone can and does defeat sin and its ability to control and damn us. This He did by an act more awesome than the prowess of evil. God actually became one of us and took upon himself the role of condemned sinner; He adopted the task of defeating sin's power by dying under the penalty that was rightfully ours. By so doing, He set us free from sin—*from the guilt and punishment of sin and from the control over us of sin's power.* From His act of self-giving, we learn that (1) self-sacrifice (not greed, pride, and envy) defeats sin; (2) dying for others leads to victory; (3) only in the individual's personal reconciliation with God is sin's power ever vanquished; (4) sin and its punishment, too massive for our shoulders, must be borne by another; and (5) humble suffering has great strength. We also learn that if we receive Him as our own answer, He will do what no psychologist, psychiatrist, professor, physicist, philosopher, or politician—no human being, including ourselves—can ever do. He will give us absolute triumph over sin's power and its consequences.

The Case Examples

This kind of writing creates a conflict for both writer and reader. It is clearly important to include narratives, examples from the lives of real persons to clarify and make concrete the ideas presented. However, events from actual cases cannot simply be presented as they happened. Therefore it is necessary to make creative changes, combinations, generalizations, and other devices to protect people. The stories are not quite true because of this. Yet they are true, not as to the precise alignment of the facts portrayed, but as to the meanings they are meant to instance and illustrate. This means that you cannot discover someone you know or even yourself in the pages to follow. So don't try.

The Sin Test

Is it possible to diagnose our sins? The idea is not so wild as it may sound. Remember that for sin there exists an explicit God-given remedy: participation by faith in the atoning work of Jesus Christ. If psychologists have steered us away from the truth by labeling every deviant behavior "sick," it makes sense to consider whether regaining the biblical perspective on sin might give us a more honest understanding of the situation. Taking one step in that direction, I created a test for diagnosing seven sinful traits. What this test yields is a profile that reveals a person's scores for *pride, envy, anger, greed, sloth, lust,* and *gluttony* compared with the scores of a "norm group" (one hundred Christian workers). I devised this test for the purpose of studying such questions as these: Are certain psychological diagnoses, in actuality, secular labels for certain sin traits? Might some others be partially caused by specific sins or aggravated by certain sin habits? My experiments revealed evidence supporting the connection between psychopathology—the study of behavioral dysfunction via mental disorder—and sin. The Sin Test can be found in the first appendix; there you may administer it to yourself if you choose. Also, in a chapter on each of these seven sins there will be sample questions. For now the considerations are (1) How can we examine ourselves using the Seven Deadly Sins system? and (2) How is Christ Jesus the cure we need for our disorders, for our own deadly sins?

Considering What Sin Is

First, let's define the little word *sin.* Not giving the term any thought at all, we generally presume that sins are immoral actions or immoral thoughts or fantasies. Now, the idea that sin is wicked behavior or wicked thinking is not wrong, but it is only part of the story. Consider another facet: Biblical writers understood sin as something larger than an action or thought; they recognized an actual *power* inside us, a *driving motivation.* This drive *influences* our actions, but it is not identical with actions.

Theologians have described it as an *inclination* to disobey God and exalt self, a *disposition* that is a part of every human being. This *penchant* is sometimes called a "power" because it exerts motivational force on thought, feeling, will, and action. We have this innate potency at work within us, "lying at the door," as God put it to Cain. For a thorough discussion of this concept of sin, consult chapters six and seven of Romans.

Some Sins Are Habits

Glenn had learned how to use his free will enthusiastically and energetically to give up his adulterous porn viewing, replacing it with certain behaviors incompatible with sexual sin. (I'll explain this later.) The plan worked quite well for five weeks, but then he missed an appointment, and I had a hunch the reason was not good. It wasn't. He had slipped back into the old groove. *Groove* is a very good word for this and other sins because it illustrates certain aspects of habits. Some sins are single behavior episodes; *habits* are grooves. Once we get into a groove, leaving it requires God's help and our best efforts. Without these, we retain and repeat certain kinds of sin. The Seven Deadly Sins are all habits; they are not rare, occasional, or one-time transgressions. By repeating them again and again, usually obtaining some kind of reward (reinforcement), we etch the groove deeper into ourselves and make it harder to stop.

We can all name hundreds of sinful acts, so what's special about *these* sins? Well, in one sense, they aren't the sort of things we usually think of when we hear the word *sin*. We usually think of sin as a deviant action we perform, an evil deed we do, a degenerate thought we harbor, a forbidden transgression we commit, a vile fantasy we entertain. Remarkably, however, not one of the Seven Deadly Sins is a single, separate sinful behavior—not one is an individual action, such as killing or stealing. Instead, all of them are what psychologists refer to as *traits*.

How is a trait different from a single behavior episode? Traits are not events; they are not acts or thoughts, but *characteristics*, enduring *habits*, under-the-skin *inclinations* to behave in certain ways. Some well-known traits are *generosity, optimism, verbosity,* and *courage.* Traits are enduring behavioral motivations, leanings toward acting in a given way. In this respect the Seven Deadly Sins are also personality *traits,* but with emphasis on moral and spiritual factors. It would be awkward to use pride, envy, greed, and so on to denote specific acts; we can't appropriately speak of doing a lust or committing a sloth. But can we use these terms to describe a person's personality? Of course we can. If someone asks you to describe Jones, you might reply, "Jones is a proud man—always trying to get attention." How about Smith? "Smith is greedy. Although he has plenty of money, he never stops worrying about how to get more."

The Seven Deadly Sins are character traits that seem to be pervasive throughout humanity. They are present in all human beings, although their relative strengths are different in each individual. Some of you might be asking whether it is possible to determine not to be proud or envious or lustful, for example, and then achieve success. Or are we all doomed to cling to these sinful traits whether we want to or not? Can we get anywhere by trying with all our might, by using our wills? Do you believe in something people call "willpower"?

Does Your Will Have Freedom?

Some psychologists believe that our wills are not free to choose. They insist that we do what we do because of our genetic endowment (our heredity) or our experiences (our past), not because we have something called free will by which we choose our own actions. One famous behaviorist even wrote a widely read (and seriously flawed) book entitled *Beyond Freedom and Dignity,*[1] in which he argued that human behavior cannot be called free because it is altogether determined by the environment. If this is true, he concluded, then people don't deserve to be valued or reviled for doing what they do—they can't help their choices. The argument is actually an old one among philosophers, one that, according to most, cannot be logically resolved. Immanuel Kant, for instance, showed that by using *reason* (or *logic*) one could prove the case for *either* freedom or determinism.

Well, then, what does the Bible say about this? Here we must make our way carefully lest we wander away from the pure teaching of God's Word. Let's begin by noting that believers have been set free by Christ Jesus so that they are able to exercise freedom in their behavioral choices. "Set free" from what? As I understand Scripture, without being born again of water and of the Spirit, human beings lack the power to make right choices. This is because without faith, their choices cannot satisfy God's criteria (or in the language of Scripture, "Without faith it is impossible to please God" [Hebrews 11:6 NIV]).

People without faith are said to be "in bondage." *Can* they choose morally correct behavior? Certainly, and the world is better off when they do. But so long as these choices are not driven by the engine of God's Holy Spirit through faith in Christ Jesus, they spring from self-interest and in the end have no spiritual value. People trying to defeat sin in this way are locked into self and the tyranny of self-love. Believers are people who have been set free from this bondage and made able to cooperate with God himself in His work of improving them.

The Seven Deadly Sins

Studying the Seven Deadly (or Capital) Sins has for more than one and a half millennia served believers (and even some unbelievers) as a mirror for the soul. Far from being a haphazard list of evil deeds, the catalog of seven sins actually provides a system for spiritual and moral inventory. These seven sins are all discussed in the New Testament, and recently a popular evangelical television ministry focused on them in a special program, which featured several new books on the seven sins.

They are called "deadly" because they can become habits strong enough to take over one's character and so impress themselves that the person wanders away from God's gift of life in pursuit of one or more of them. They are called "capital" (from the Latin word for "head," *caput*) since each of them is the head of a list of other sins that spring from them. Here is the list, in English and in Latin, with a Scripture reference for each. The order here is mine:

- Pride, *superbia*: "For all that is in the world, the lust of the flesh and the lust of the eyes and the *pride* of life, is not of the Father but is of the world" (1 John 2:16).
- Envy, *invidia*: "So put away all malice and all guile and insincerity and *envy* and all slander" (1 Peter 2:1).
- Anger, *ira*: "I desire then that in every place the men should pray, lifting holy hands without *anger* or quarreling" (1 Timothy 2:8).
- Greed, *avaritia*: "Do you not know that the unrighteous will not inherit the kingdom of God? Do not be deceived; neither the immoral, nor idolaters, nor adulterers, nor sexual perverts, nor thieves, nor the *greedy*, nor drunkards, nor revilers, nor robbers will inherit the kingdom of God" (1 Corinthians 6:9–10).
- Sloth, *acedia*: "But his master answered him, 'You wicked and *slothful* servant!' " (Matthew 25:26).
- Lust, *luxuria*: "The Lord knows how to . . . keep the unrighteous under punishment until the day of judgment, and especially those who indulge in the *lust* of defiling passion" (2 Peter 2:9–10).
- Gluttony, *gula*: This word does not occur in the English translations I have reviewed. However, the concept of the sin itself is described in several passages. For example, see Philippians 3:19: "Whose end is destruction, *whose God is their belly,* and whose glory is in their shame, who mind earthly things" (KJV).

Anything that has proved to be useful for more than sixteen hundred years of pastoral care deserves our attention; such durability tells us we have found something of special interest. What could be so engaging about the Seven Deadly Sins? To begin with, they yield profound insight into personality, more profound in some ways than those of secular psychological systems, particularly because of the unquenchable vitality of the truth they uncover. It is not only the near-universality of their fascination but also the powerful insights they descriptively and prescriptively reveal about human behavior that grab our attention.

I have been pondering this assembly of seven behavioral traits for over thirty years, and I have noted that even people who have no particular religious beliefs seem to find exploring these characteristics a remarkably useful procedure. Those readers who are participators in the joyous mysteries of the Christian faith will find themselves both curious to learn more about their particular deadly sins and desirous of a stirring for fresh renewal, a calling from their hearts to the heart of God for divine aid in the battle.

Although a major value to be gained from this study will be self-assessment and self-diagnosis, a deeper understanding of our sins and the part they play in generating our pain will come into light as well. As we have seen, unless we obtain a thorough awareness of our own sins, we won't care much about God's announcement of divine power for overcoming our own monstrous, repulsive moral hang-ups. Why? Because we either won't see them as such, or we will believe that there really isn't much we can do about them anyway. Those forms of Christianity that say we can never have victory over the power of sin have it wrong. They need to back off their numbing proclamations that emphasize defeat and ultimately despair. In God through Christ we study our sins only to gain mastery over the depressing drudgery of waking up every day to face our same old sinful habits and attitudes—the ugly traits that sometimes seem to never go away. *Perfection?* We will achieve it in Christ Jesus, but only when God sees fit to call us home. *Progress?* That is to be a prime characteristic of our lives right now.

How to Make Progress

Two friends of mine, Mark and Corinne Loe, laid seven huge bonfires in the woods, named them *Pride, Envy, Anger, Greed, Sloth, Lust,* and *Gluttony,* and with appropriate prayer and truthful self-talk, set each one ablaze, symbolizing the destruction of these sin drives deep within themselves. True enough, bonfires in the woods won't defeat sin, no matter what names we give them. They did, however, serve as powerful symbols for Mark and Corinne. We cannot in our own strength, with only our human faculties, believe in Christ Jesus or come to a sin-destroying relationship with Him unless the Holy Spirit works faith in our hearts. Certainly our wills, unaided by the Holy Spirit, are weak and helpless in the war on sin. But since believers are empowered by the indwelling of the Spirit of God, they can *choose* to light the blazing fires of regenerate will and work effectively toward change in behavior and character.

As you strain to understand and change your own sinful ways, you will meet a difficulty at the heart of Christianity itself, the only religion (other than the Judaism of the Old Testament) that poses this paradoxical conundrum. Simply put, *only God* can defeat the tyrannical power of our sinfulness; but *we ourselves* are to turn away from our sins, no matter how ingrained they have become and regardless of how much we have come to rely on sinning. *On the one hand,* God's Word reveals that human efforts cannot possibly win this war; blood sacrifice must be offered. This is the lesson taught by the requirements of Old Testament worship and its New Covenant fulfillment in Jesus. Only the rich blood of the Son of God, the Son of Man—only His suffering and death—is big enough to deflect the flaming rays of God's wrath from the sinner to the Substitute. *On the other hand,* though it appears contradictory at first, the task of choosing right over wrong is ours. We are told to "sin not." Are we helpless pawns? Are we capable of defeating evil on our own? Does God do it all? Is it His job or ours? An arresting comment by Paul strikingly places the paradox before our eyes: "Work out your own salvation with fear and trembling; for God is at work in you, both to will and to work for his good pleasure" (Philippians 2:12–13).

Can We Stop Sin in Its Tracks?

Can we work out our own salvation and get rid of sin *by ourselves?* No. The drive to keep on sinning seems unstoppable.

Even Paul confessed that he often found himself doing evil precisely when he wanted to do good. When it comes to sin, people can't "just say no"; that isn't the whole picture. The self-offering of God had to occur. He came to "save us from our sins," not merely to save us from the *punishment* but from the *grip* of sinning. By faith in the death and resurrection of Christ, believers are given the Holy Spirit, indwelling their own spirits to free them from that trap, to create renewed drives, and to empower them to replace sin with new behaviors.

To do our part in all this, we must understand that sins get their hold on us by becoming habits. We must examine ourselves to discover where this habituating of sin has occurred in us. Such understanding can lead to repentance, our Spirit-led reaction to meeting up with our own sinfulness.

Three Important Rules for Success

Following are three indispensable principles for success against sin, particularly habit-sins like the ones discussed in this study. Memorize the rules and develop the habit of applying them regularly as you create your own bonfires for sin.

1. *The principle of checking your Spirit-given internal speech.* People differ in the development of their ability to do this. Some have a lifelong habit of paying attention to externals: outward circumstances, what someone else does or says, frustrations and irritants in the environment. Others have read or heard teaching about paying attention to their own self-talk (internal speech), and they have taught themselves the habit of checking within. This can be confusing at first, because you will discover two opposing themes in your own mind. One strain of self-talk will make the case for acting proud or envious or otherwise wicked; the other will oppose it and argue the case for defeating the *sin-advocate* inside you. The first theme is generated by our enemies: the devil, the world, and our own sinful nature. The second theme is communicated by the Holy Spirit. It is the voice of our own reborn, truth-instructed conscience. No matter how faint this second voice seems, no matter how slight and thin the

desire to be a better person, it deserves your attention because it reflects your true and sincere wish to please God by obedience to His will. It is this second theme you must look for by asking yourself, *"What is my Holy Spirit-inspired, Word-instructed spirit urging me to do or not do right now?"* And listen carefully to the counsel of the Spirit of God within.

When you have retrieved the answer, repeat it to yourself. Repeat it again and again. Argue for the truth and defeat the fallacious arguments of lust, pride, greed, and other sins. Drown out the voices of enemies and overcome them with the truth of God. Resolutely let it control you, using all the strength of your spiritual muscles.

So the principle of checking your Spirit-given internal speech is this: "When I sense that something is not quite right, I will check my Spirit-given internal speech and follow its leading."

2. *The principle of choosing incompatible behavior.* You may have noticed that some actions make it nearly impossible to perform certain other actions at the same time. Some examples: playing golf at the same time you are worshiping in church; eating a heavy meal while you are exercising or weightlifting; smoking a cigarette while you are inside a "No Smoking" workplace. Similarly, it is difficult to do some wrong acts while you are deeply involved in doing certain other right deeds. It's hard to treat your spouse badly while you are energetically occupied with meeting her emotional needs; you can hardly be planning to bring down someone you envy and dislike while at the same time studying the impossible-to-ignore words of Jesus' Sermon on the Mount; you can't be out drinking with your rowdy companions at the same time you are home in bed. *Doing wrong is often so incompatible with doing right that choosing one eliminates the possibility of the other.* What a simple principle and yet how effective! To gain ground in the battle against selfish greed, you must not only resolutely stop being greedy; even more availing is to practice giving generously for the good of others in need. To make it more challenging for yourself to envy your friend,

do as Martin Luther suggested: "Help him to improve and protect his property and business."

If you can't think what to do in a given situation, go to Principle #1 and check your Spirit-given internal speech. So the principle of choosing incompatible behavior is this: "I will make a habitual practice of using my will to choose speech and actions that make it more difficult to let my pride (or greed or other sin habit) control my thoughts and behavior."

3. *The principle of zealous determination.* No doubt we can all make pious choices of a sort. Sometimes we make good choices grudgingly. I was trying to show Grant, a client, how he could work to improve his marriage using one of Dr. Willard Harley's principles. "Grant, you can make things much better if you will dedicate yourself to meeting Serenity's emotional needs. Up until now, you may have given little thought to her desires. To improve things at home, you must resolve to work hard at it from now on. Are you willing to do that?"

"Yeah, I guess I'd better," he answered, with very little enthusiasm.

Not what I had in mind. If we want to make headway against our sins, we have to apply the principle of zealous determination.

Most of us have experienced choosing to do right without enthusiasm. And there are times when such choices are only reasonable. When the question arises whether to stop at a red traffic light or not, the correct choice can be made without any special enthusiasm. It would be difficult, maybe even dangerous, to *zealously* stop at red lights—plain old stopping without much enthusiasm works just fine. *Zeal* describes a different style—one of resolute determination, of energetic decisiveness. The word has a firm, loud, deep sound, like the booming of a bass drum in a parade or the most emphatic thunder crash you can imagine. Zeal doesn't get much play in contemporary speech because we carry on so much of our life without it. Often our choices to win against sin are correct choices, but they fail because we lack zeal. So when you choose to battle a deadly sin, remember to make the choice with *zealous determination*: "I *WILL* give this sin a fight!"

Do Sinners Have a Choice?

Perhaps you haven't had much success with your own sinful traits and you wonder whether some of us are doomed to cling to these bad habits whether we want to or not. You ask, "Can we really get anywhere by moving forward with zealous determination, by trying with all our might, by exercising our will?"

You *can* win against sin. First, you must be a believing Christian, committed to obeying Christ. Second, you must want to win against your own deadly sins. Working with the material in this book, you will find your understanding increasing, and you will begin to think about the extent to which one or more of these sins has gained a foothold in your life. You will find various assessment tools to help you: (1) a list at the end of this chapter enables you to evaluate yourself on each of the Seven Deadly Sins; (2) a sample Sin Test on an individual sin appears at the end of each subsequent chapter; and (3) appendix 1 contains the complete Sin Test, together with directions for scoring and interpreting it.

But understanding alone is not enough for victory. Remember to practice the three principles discussed above: (1) the principle of checking your Spirit-given internal speech, replacing the bad with the good, the distorted with the truth; (2) the principle of choosing incompatible behavior; and (3) the principle of making moral choices with zealous determination.

How to Use This Book

You may have any number of aims in reading this study of the Seven Deadly Sins. Most common for many readers may be the goal of *true self-understanding*. Make sure you realize that psychological self-analysis, while often useful, remains partial and incomplete because it usually eliminates the domain of ethics and morals. You can use this book to learn which of these traits are more dominant, and therefore troublesome, in your personality. Such knowledge can then open the way for you to work with the Holy Spirit toward liberation.

To help you in reaching better insight, as well as to aid you in evaluating your progress, you will find a list at the end of this chapter that briefly describes each of the Seven Deadly Sins. Using these descriptions, along with your present level of understanding, you may assign numbers from 1 to 7, according to the influence of each sin on your behavior. A sin with the strongest conceivable influence on you would be given a *1*; the weakest, a *7*. This tool will provide a record of your self-assessment *before* you study the book. The same list will appear again at the end of the book, where you will want to assign numbers from 1 to 7 to each of your own sin traits. Compare the two for changes you may have made during your study. This will be a completely subjective exercise based on your own prayerful sense of conviction.

For a somewhat more objective method of developing insight, I have included ten true/false questions at the end of each chapter. These will be relevant to the particular sin covered in the chapter. Along the way, you will encounter instruction and case presentations; through these you can learn how to achieve practical, everyday victory over powerful sin habits.

Again, the complete Sin Test appears in appendix 1, for those who would like to work through it.

Try a Preliminary Personal Checkup Now

In the next seven chapters you will learn the meanings of each one of the Seven Deadly Sins. Again, the cure is repentance, confession, and the faith to trust the power of the cross of Jesus Christ to save us from our sins. You should gain a much clearer understanding of yourself and your own most significant sin traits. Before you go any further, try this personal checkup. It will help you to get an initial overview, as well as determine how you understand your own sin problems at this point in time. As mentioned, after you have read about the sins in detail, you can do the checkup again to see if you have a new or altered understanding of sin.

Individually Rank-Ordering the Seven Deadly Sin Traits

You can use the following for rank-ordering yourself on the Seven Capital Sins. The trait on which you consider yourself to score highest is #1. The one on which you are lowest is #7. If you are ranking a friend or a spouse, use the same system. Feel free to make copies of this form if you wish to share it with someone else.

_____ PRIDE: Being desirous of occupying first place; seeking to have authority over others; detesting being under authority or external restraints; overestimating self or one's own abilities and gifts; exhibiting blindness to good qualities in others; showing contempt for others; being anxious to get credit; having presumptuous ambition; taking on tasks without the ability to perform them; thriving on praise and recognition; boasting or faking self-deprecation; being shocked with the misdeeds and faults of others; being self-satisfied; being thrilled or enamored with one's own spiritual and moral achievements; being strongly opinionated, inflexible, or argumentative; chafing under the rule and sovereignty of God.

_____ ENVY: Habitually being in competition with others; feeling unhappy when another gets a break; being glad when others (especially those perceived as "equals") have setbacks or troubles; losing "self-esteem" when another is perceived as having more (spirituality, attractiveness, popularity, intelligence, material rewards—anything) than oneself; desiring to expose defects in others; frequently interpreting others' words and deeds as bad; persistently tuning in to compare self with others—their qualities, possessions, achievements, etc.

_____ ANGER: Having a strong desire for revenge; cultivating and harboring resentment; thinking about getting even; arguing, quarreling, fighting; being primarily silent and sullen; being sarcastic, cynical, insulting, critical; frequently being indignant; desiring harm for others; considering it right to "settle the score."

_____ GREED: Wanting to accumulate material things just for the sake of possessing them; cheating, lying, or stealing to gain or hang on to things; being tightfisted and retentive; being excessively thrifty; being overcautious about spending; hating to give; being stingy; being callous toward the needy; hating to pay debts, avoiding repayment whenever possible; feeling excessive distress at small losses; finding it hard to trust God to provide for needs.

_____ SLOTH: Being sorrowful in spirit and mind; finding it difficult to have hope; believing effort and work are too difficult; procrastinating, putting off attending to important matters; deciding prayer or worship is too hard; being sluggish and heavy; having a will that is weak; feeling it is useless to try to break bad habits; often investing self in trivial activities; constantly seeking bodily ease and comfort; preferring idleness to activity; being sad and spiritually worn out; drifting along in mediocrity; being dissatisfied and angry with God for not giving feelings of peace, consolation, and happiness.

_____ LUST: Being regularly preoccupied with sexual pleasure, thoughts, and fantasies; thinking about sexual pleasure to the exclusion of other things; looking at, touching, embracing, or engaging in intercourse with illicit or forbidden sexual objects or activities; persisting in excessive interest, conversations, or jokes abut sex.

_____ GLUTTONY: Overindulging in pursuit of worldly pleasure; eating too much; eating too fast; being preoccupied with food; drinking alcohol too often or too much; being finicky or choosy about food or drink; overly investing in the enjoyment of gourmet foods, wines, literature, music, the arts; embracing pursuits that do not meet fulfillment in God.

If you have rated yourself on this list, save it for comparison with the self-assessments you may choose to take after studying the next seven chapters.

Notes

1. B. F. Skinner, *Beyond Freedom and Dignity* (New York: Knopf, 1971).

Chapter 2

Pride—The Root of the Root Sins

The most shocking, painful, annihilating, devastating, crushing, humiliating, mortifying verbal swat I ever received was laid on me by my own dear mother. She had always rewarded my performances with unbridled praise, so I was anticipating her customary warm approval. But this time my expectations were shattered.

I had been the master of ceremonies for an evening of entertainment at our church, a show produced by our youth group. The idea was copied from the popular *Truth or Consequences* radio/TV program, and we invited adults in the audience to participate as contestants. I would ask the contestant a question—one nobody could answer, such as, "How many penguins are there in the Arctic Circle?" Then, when they hadn't told the truth (which was every time, because the game was purposely rigged with impossible questions), they would have to pay the consequences by doing something embarrassing.

Trying my best to imitate Ralph Edwards (the TV star emcee), I acted smart, witty, really cool—I thought. I paraded up and down the stage, wising off at other kids' parents, imagining I was a brilliant sixteen-year-old protégé who would soon be featured on a show that would sweep the nation. Get the picture? I was impressed with myself.

Now, in the car on the way home, I waited for Mother to tell me I had done it all splendidly. But she was strangely silent. At last, when she spoke, she told me straight out: I had embarrassed her. She saw what I had refused to see: a smart-aleck kid with an inflated ego, preening and showing off—"Look, everybody, at how clever I can be!" At that moment my mother was not thrilled that this impudent kid was her son. What she saw instead of deft cleverness and shining intelligence was a huge case of *pride*. And it was not a pretty sight.

After that neither of us said anything. The ride home seemed to take forever. Deflated, I went to my room to nurse my wounds. I stretched out on my bed and thought about the show, trying to recall what I had said and done—defending myself, justifying my performance, making myself righteous. But it was no use. Mother was right and I knew it. I had blown it; I was a failure. And as my own arrogance appeared to me in its true repulsive light, I became depressed. The pain stayed around for a while.

What was the sorrow I felt—clinical depression? An illness? Something to be treated with medication and/or psychotherapy? Or was it a gift, a strict but loving teacher provided by God for my benefit? Would it be more accurate to see my sadness as appropriate, like what Paul labeled "godly sorrow" because it did his readers good?

Today, after three decades of practice as a clinical psychologist, if I had that same sixteen-year-old as a client, I would not diagnose his sorrow as depression unless it developed complications and continued for a longer time. Technically, a blue mood can't be diagnosed as a depressive illness until it has hung around for at least two weeks. I understand now, even though I was naive and very young, that the pain I experienced was created by a deadly sin: pride. By the time I felt the pain, my bubble had burst, my ego was wounded. But the grief did me good.

Here's how it worked: When God, speaking through my mother, punched a big hole in my arrogance, my deflated pride changed to painful self-devaluation. Instead of "What a great showman I am," it was "What a dumb jerk! I *see* it now. I really blew it when I told myself I was making entertainment history; I was actually making the crowd wish they were home in bed!"

Could the depressive *misbeliefs*—"I'm no good," "I'm a failure," "I don't like myself very well," and so forth—in certain instances be nothing more than the backside of pride? *Punctured* pride? Could my funk have endured for weeks and months instead of hours? Of course. And in another person, maybe a person who had previously experienced a series of losses, that very thing might happen. I could have been a different youngster, one whose genetic endowment had predisposed me to enduring more lingering consequences. Nevertheless, I conclude that it is possible for symptoms like depression, compulsive tendencies, and anxiety to grow out of pride.

Look more deeply at the sin of pride—what is it, anyway? In its essence, it is more than just thinking of ourselves more highly than we ought to think (Romans 12:3). It certainly *includes* an unrealistically inflated self-concept. But at its core, pride is more evil, more perverse even than this. For the core false belief of pride is nothing less than an individual's conviction that "I really ought to be God. If only I could take God's place, how I would change things!"

St. John Cassian: Pride and Autonomy

St. John Cassian, who in A.D. 415 founded the first monasteries in Europe, has strong medicine to prescribe for us today. Cassian was one of the earliest Christian writers to discuss the Seven Deadly Sins, and I hope you will ponder his words carefully, for they can reveal pride for what it is: the only sin (says Cassian) so serious it calls forth resistance and opposition from God himself! To prove his point, he cites James 4:6 and 1 Peter 5:5, both of which warn their readers, "God resisteth the proud, but giveth grace unto the humble"(KJV).

How great is the evil of pride, that it rightly has no angel, nor other virtues opposed to it, but God Himself as its adversary! It should be noted that it is never said of those who are entangled in other sins that they have God resisting them; I mean it is not said that God is opposed "to the gluttonous, fornicators, passionate, or covetous," but only "to the proud." For those sins react only on those who commit them, or seem to be committed against those who share in them, i.e., against other men; but this one has more properly to do with God, and therefore it is especially right that it should have Him opposed to it.[1]

Contemporary Christianity sometimes dodges the real issue. Does your preacher talk to you about "problems" so as to avoid the word sin? Do some sermons resemble psychotherapy rather than sin-cure? John Cassian dares to say that the deadly sin of pride is "an evil." This may sound strange to your modern-day ear; you may have been taught that of all desirable traits, proud self-esteem must be at the pinnacle. So why is pride so bad? It is especially dangerous because of its core, because of what you always find when you peel away layer after layer of our arrogant attitudes. Down in its heart of hearts, our pride generates lethal animosity *against God* and promotes the belief that "I ought to be, can be, and by right *am* my own god." *Every* person's proud heart, in some way or in every way, wants to be in charge, wants to displace God and move into primacy, taking first place. This illusion is called autonomy.

"It's My Life and I'm in Charge!"

A seventeen-year-old woman saw me to help untangle her jumbled life. She was young to be sure, but about all kinds of life experiences she could already say, "Been there, done that." She had just been released from a corrections institution. Her offense: stealing mail to find money. She had recently given up her second child for adoption and was trying to raise her first. She took to drinking, promiscuity, and drugs at fourteen, bearing her first child at fifteen. She and her current boyfriend

planned to marry, and I suggested she might make a start re-
building her life by waiting to sleep with him until after the wed-
ding. Her response: "I don't believe *that* much in God."

Examine her answer carefully. She realized that there is a
Being called God, but she had no intention of allowing Him to
take away her autonomy. Autonomy: It's the hallucination of the
stubborn heart that says, "It's my life and I'm the boss—nobody
can tell me what to do." At least her reply was said straight-out,
unlike the hypocritical heart that not only hangs onto autonomy
in the face of God but at the same time pretends to have surren-
dered all.

At War With God

Human pride is the same war with God that was first fought
by Satan and his allies at a point now shrouded in the mists of
history. They are still at it, working to overcome God, to take
His place, and to be exalted over all. John Milton captured the
original act of rebellious pride in a breathtaking poem called
Paradise Lost. Read it carefully; take your time; get the picture.

> Th' infernal Serpent . . . his pride
> Had cast him out from Heaven, with all his host
> Of rebel Angels, by whose aid, aspiring
> To set himself in glory above his peers,
> He trusted to have equaled the Most High,
> If he opposed, and with ambitious aim
> Against the throne and monarchy of God,
> Raised impious war in Heaven. . . .[2]

Is Pride a Thought Disorder?

The creature believed he could win a war against God because he imagined himself at least as magnificent as his Creator.
Psychologically speaking, this is a delusion. Put the way Milton's epic poem describes it (and the way the moral theologians
write about it), pride, more than any other sin, tends to involve

disordered thinking. For most of us, our proud behavior does not amount to psychosis, but it can—and in some cases does—involve serious thought disorder.

If a patient says, "I am Hitler," the psychiatrist prescribes antipsychotic medication. If he comes right out and declares, "I am God," the same therapy will likely be administered. Yet what if a person doesn't put it quite that directly but instead simply insists that nobody has a right to tell him what to do? This notion is as much a factual error as if he were to declare himself to be the fourth person in the Godhead. Surely it would be wise to search for a deeper connection between psychiatric diagnoses involving thought disorder and sin. After we look more closely at the pride syndrome, I will describe some experimental results of my own that may suggest, on empirical grounds, that this deeper connection exists.

Protecting Our Status

At first blush we may prefer to believe we are "sick" rather than "sinful." Perhaps this explains the tendency in Christian churches to soften phraseology and trade concepts with psychology. We talk about mental illness, sometimes (or often, or always) replacing the biblical term *sin*. If our plight really is illness, we usually cannot be made responsible for its ravages; if our plight is sin, we must take the blame. It's not easy to search out and own up to the depth of our own pride.

A new *Methodist Book of Worship* has just appeared from the United Kingdom. Excluded is the traditional Episcopal/Methodist "Prayer of Humble Access" at Holy Communion, which begins, "We do not presume to come to this your table, merciful Lord. . . ." The committee thought the prayer was too "grovelly." Said a spokesman, "We do not want people to be brought down at this holy moment and be reminded that they are a sinner." They didn't want to confront spiritual pride, and very likely they expected such a prayer might meet with resistance from contemporary worshipers, many of whom have come to believe they are smooth characters with nothing to be humble about.

However, in order to be free, we need to chase this enemy out of the bushes and get a close-up of what our own pride looks like. *There is no replacement for this necessity.*

The Tragic Results of Pride Run Amuck

The classic study of conflicted pride, the pride that tries to take over God's place, is *Crime and Punishment* by Fyodor Dostoevsky. Raskolnikov, a university student, conceives a plan to murder an old woman, a pawnbroker. She is covetous, mean, and of no use to anyone, so he argues to himself that she truly deserves to die. Then, her money, in his hands, might do some good. He could use it to help his destitute sister and the poverty-stricken Sonia, a girl forced by love to sacrifice herself in prostitution to save her starving family. Raskolnikov begins to think how murdering this worthless, evil old woman will remove a harmful organism from society, stop the evil she has been doing, free her money to save impoverished people, and enable the superior person who murdered her to thus serve humanity. Convincing himself that he is that "superior person," he strikes the old woman twice with the blunt side of an ax and takes her money.

Raskolnikov adopts his reasoning from the German philosopher Friedrich Nietzsche, who announced to the world that God is dead because He was too soft and "groveling." Nietzsche argued that history now awaited the appearance of God's replacement, the "Superman." This ideal human being would be so strong, so superior, that he would have the right to determine who may live and thrive and who is useless and ought to be destroyed. "If God is dead, then Superman is God."[3] So reasoned Nietzsche, so reasoned Raskolnikov, and *so reasons pride at its core.*

Dostoevsky's immortal novel shows Nietzsche's ideal to be nothing but human pride run amuck: rebellion. Some readers will say, "What a curious notion. But what has it to do with me?

I don't think I'm 'Superman.' All I want is a little more self-esteem. I never think of wanting to be God." Oh no? What, then, *are* we thinking when we tell God what to do and complain when He does His will instead of ours? When we think how much better the world would be if we were running its affairs? When in some of our nearly atheistic moments we allow ourselves the thought that the world is so horrible there couldn't be a good, loving, and just God? Making self preeminent is the core of the deadly sin of pride.

Pictures of Pride

Pride comes in diverse packages with numerous subtraits. Ask yourself whether your troubles come from some of pride's unattractive excrescences: trying to be noticed, craving attention, itching for compliments, hungering for praise, needing to be important, hating to be "grovelly," detesting the idea of being submissive, loathing the idea of admitting to wrongdoing, being strongly opinionated, being impervious to reason, being argumentative, demanding your way, wanting control over others, flaunting your individual rights, refusing advice, being defensive, being critical yet resenting criticism, being thoughtless, being inconsiderate, being presumptuous, being self-righteous, imagining you are your own source, over-inflating your own abilities, devaluing others, boasting, being inordinately anxious about what others might think of you, worrying lest others talk about you behind your back, being oversensitive, thinking you have excellences you don't have, exhibiting hypocrisy, holding on to certain kinds of low self-esteem. Pride is a *huge* sin. Take time to read this paragraph again, because becoming cured—changing into a better man or woman—must begin with facing what needs to change.

All six of the other deadly sins—envy, anger, greed, sloth, lust, and gluttony—are grounded in *pride*, rebellion against the rule of the King of Kings. This is because sin, by definition, is transgression against God's law.

Atheism and Pride

I don't imagine that many of my readers are hardcore atheists, but even believers can have "atheistic moments," instances when they become frustrated with God and create a rift between Him and themselves by experimenting with dangerous denial of His presence or His love. Atheists typically claim that they are humble seekers of truth and that they love truth so ardently they simply cannot believe in a loving Supreme Being when the world is so full of injustice and suffering. They say they have seen no evidence that there is a God, and that if there is He must be either weak or evil. Some of these unbelievers go out of their way to be polite, kind, and good to others. By so doing they attempt to prove that they are better than deeply convinced believers (often depicted by atheists as rigid, opinionated, heartless, and irrational, those whom a certain politician has described as "extra-chromosome Christians").

But the word *atheist* literally means "without God." Atheism is never truly humble; rather, unmasked, it is extreme pride because, like Friedrich Nietzsche, it *attempts to do away with God and exalts self.* Like all the subtraits of pride, this one makes *self* foremost. On my prideful climb to the top, I find it necessary to push down every other contender for first place.

Controlling

Are you a controller? *Control* is a most glaring exhibition of pride; a constraining desire for control may be totally invisible to the sinner, though it is obvious to others. This compelling force pushes for power and authority over others, even if one tries to hide it from oneself and everyone else. It lurks deep down in the heart, awaiting another ugly manifestation.

Opinionated

People who are *opinionated* simply cannot stand being wrong. They will not give up until you agree with them. If you persist in honest disagreement, they take it as a personal affront. They often frame their opinions in a format that sounds like the final word. They seldom add something like, "Of course, this is only my opinion." Why should they listen to someone else's reasoning when in their hearts they see no difference between their beliefs and indubitable facts?

Impervious to Reason

Some prideful characters are so rigidly opinionated that even if they listen to reason, it has no effect because they have become calloused and *impervious to reason*, like Pharaoh, who repeatedly hardened his heart in the face of truth. For some of these people, facts and logic have so little importance that they do not actually argue; instead they quarrel, call names, and hurl insults at those who disagree with them. Driven by an overweening ambition to be more right than anyone else, their fear of being bested by someone in an argument forces them to keep repeating their opinions in a louder and more combative tone.

Quarreling, Combative, Disagreeable, and Critical

Verbal quarreling for some proud persons is very nearly their only conversational style. Are they *combative*? Disagreeable? Absolutely. If you say, *tomayto*, they say, *tomahto*; if you say, *potayto*, they say, *potahto*. If you say, "It's been a lovely spring," they say, "It's been too stormy." If you say, "That was a good sermon," they say, "I suppose, if you like that sort of thing." Such people regularly become featured guests on certain TV shows. If you watch, you may encounter them in on-screen shouting matches. Even when they are confronted with clear truth, they blithely ignore evidence and keep talking, growing progressively noisier so as to drown out opinions at odds with their own.

Pride makes it hard for some to *accept advice*. They reject counsel, reproof, or correction, no matter how wisely and gently it is offered. They must never let themselves admit that they might need direction, because to do so would be to occupy a more lowly position. Yet their only chance of being rescued from the evil results of their pride may be for them to tolerate the possibility of being incorrect. Instead of meeting sincere criticism with defensive argument or anger, we all need to add to our vocabulary something such as, "You might have a point. Tell me what you think. I'm all ears!"

On the other hand, a proud person, while resenting and resisting any reproach directed at him, may gladly allow himself to be very *critical* of others. Sitting high up on the throne of God (as he imagines himself), he assumes he can see clearly to remove the speck from the eye of another while remaining proudly out of touch with the log of pride in his own eye. Turning your attention to the faults of others, perhaps believing you are doing them a favor, helping them on their way through life, is a common defense mechanism. By cleverly preventing you from gaining self-understanding, this device can repeatedly deflect your gaze away from an honest look in the mirror.

Uncivil

One outcropping of pride that is characteristic of increasing numbers of people trained to despise courtesy is *incivility*: the abrasive manner of the *thoughtless* and *inconsiderate*. We have all become so accustomed to cultural breakdown since the mid–1960s that we may not even remember when boorish behavior was unacceptable. Recently a friend told me about his encounter with a graceless buffoon in a shop where he was waiting for his turn in the checkout line. The other man sidled up to him and said, "I want you to know that when we get up to the counter, I'm going ahead of you. If you want to make something of it, that's fine with me."

"I Can Do Anything!"

Another kind of pride is that of presumption. This trait is an eagerness to attempt tasks that are beyond one's ability. The presumptuously proud person draws a blank when he tries to make sense out of prayers such as, "Keep back thy servant also from presumptuous sins; let them not have dominion over me: then shall I be upright, and I shall be innocent from the great transgression" (Psalm 19:13 KJV).

The proud individual really believes that he (all by himself) is capable of solving the most difficult problems, imagines that he abounds in good judgment and great wisdom, and so settles with finality the most difficult questions. Or else he may assume that his moral stamina is exceptionally great, so he walks imprudently into occasions for sin, tempting situations avoided by wiser persons who are aware of the caution issued by Paul: "Wherefore let him that thinketh he standeth take heed lest he fall" (1 Corinthians 10:12 KJV). Nor does such a person seek awareness of his own faults, as did the psalmist: "Who can understand his errors? Cleanse thou me from secret faults" (Psalm 19:12 KJV). He prefers to use other Bible passages for his prayers, like that of the Pharisee who prays, "I thank thee that I am not as other men are" (Luke 18:11 KJV).

Irrational in Thought

You may recall the suggestion that pride is related to disordered thinking. Sometimes pride generates curious, irrational ideas. For example, how often do you assume that you are the source of your own gifts and abilities? You probably know better, but wait! Even when a person knows better "officially," it's easy to slip into imagining this self-flattering nonsense—after all, it's only one more way of putting self into the place of God. People who habitually think this way magnify and exaggerate their own strong points and abilities, pushing themselves forward to teach in the church, or sing solos during services, or exhibit their prowess as theologians. Along with overestimation of their own abilities, they may frequently deprecate the contributions of others. All this follows from assuming that somehow "*I* am the one responsible for these marvelous talents and strong characteristics I am now putting at the service of the community, and I want *you* to recognize it."

Boastful

If the proud person is naive, he will candidly brag, not realizing that people usually see boasting for what it is. He never notices that God does not approve of his self-exaltation: "Why boastest thou thyself in mischief, O mighty man?" (Psalm 52:1 KJV). It might even be true that other people think he is a joke! As the same psalm puts it, "The righteous also shall see, and fear, and shall laugh at him" (v. 6). If he is more sophisticated and subtle about showing off, the boaster may skillfully nudge the conversation into areas where he thinks he has great competence. Or he may try timidly to point out his own minor faults and failings in the assurance that most people will try to buck him up by reciting his praises. It often works!

Anxious

Anxiety and pride make an interesting couple, and they go together more often than most people realize. Of course, not all anxiety springs from pride. Anxiety is a form of fear, and there are so many things to be afraid of that people can develop anxiety in all sorts of ways. But some kinds of anxiety appear to be conjoined with pride. For instance, the pride of inordinate concern about what others might think often leaves some of us anxious about other people's judgments, criticisms, or evaluations. "What will people think?" is the nagging, ever-present question. Whenever possible, these people may avoid meeting new people, opening themselves up emotionally, or mixing with groups of new acquaintances.

This social anxiety is one of the factors measured by one of the scales in the MMPI profile.[4] In administering the Sin Test, it has been interesting to discover that people who score higher on MMPI Scale 0 (a measure of introversion) also score higher on the Sin Test's Pride Scale. Although correlation between two trait measures does not prove that one trait *causes* the other, it's not difficult to imagine how the demand to be first and to be ranked higher than others might *lead* to fear of being observed and assessed.

Now, it is not wrong to prefer the good opinions of others; no particular benefit is gained if others think of you as evil, stupid, or untrustworthy. But to constantly worry lest others judge you negatively, to care so much that you avoid others or remain silent lest you say something they will consider ludicrous or lest you fall apart when you are criticized, to be always afraid that others may talk about you when you aren't present, to thrive on praise and shrink from criticism, is to try to live in an unreal world. People *will* talk about you when you are not present. You *will* sometimes be criticized. Some *will* certainly misjudge you or pick on your faults and flaws. If you handle this poorly, you may become sensitive to the most unintended slight. You might be so anxious about what others think of you that you even pretend to excel in things you don't. "Hypocrisy" is another form of pride.

Let me tell you about a client who considered his problem to be someone else's arrogance, while he insisted he himself was absolutely problem-free.

Dr. Mortenson Discovers Pride—His Own

Dr. Larry Mortenson arrived for his initial interview and entered the waiting room twenty minutes late, cell phone in hand, engaged in animated conversation, his manner of addressing my office secretary imperious. He was also quite obviously giving orders to someone at the other end of the phone line; I waited for him to finish. As I led him into my consulting room, he began explaining the reason for his visit even before we sat down.

"I don't think there is much wrong with me, actually. I'm a psychiatrist working in a clinic. I thought I would consult you about a problem caused by my chief." He seemed in a great hurry to let me know that he was a doctor and could therefore be believed when he reported that he had no psychiatric problems. At any rate, I was to understand he was not here as a regular patient in need of counseling—after all, he was a therapist himself, "in the loop," so to speak. Perhaps he had forgotten that "the healer who diagnoses and treats himself has a fool for a doctor."

He continued, "My chief of service is a woman, and I think she enjoys pushing me around. She acts more like a dictator than a colleague."

I replied, "Sounds as though your chief has a somewhat abrasive personality! That can be difficult to work with. Tell me what you would like me to do for you. How can I help?" (This man had a character problem sticking out like a bloody nose, regardless of his blatant denial. Submitting to authority was emphatically a bitter pill for him, and status and recognition mattered a great deal.)

"Well," he went on, "I have had the bad luck to work with others like her, and I haven't done very well with her type. I guess I'm just too up-front, too honest and straightforward with them. I'm finding that I need to learn more diplomatic tactics."

As Dr. Mortenson persisted in speaking, it became obvious that he had moved about from one career position to another and had not had much success at relationships with superiors in various clinics and hospitals. In addition, he had attributed his failures to others and to his own unflinching honesty in letting them know his true opinions.

Let's move ahead to his third session. At one point, I summarized, "So . . . you had a conflict with your attending physician (a principal physician supervising a patient's care) during your residency and almost got fired?"

"Well, yes. But he never understood that I knew what I was doing. I tried to tell him, but you know how arrogant some of these people can be. He wouldn't listen."

"And in your first private practice affiliation, your colleagues asked you to leave? After that you were disciplined by the board for upsetting a patient with outbursts of uncontrolled sarcastic anger?"

"That's what the patient told the board. It's true—I *was* irritated. But there were absolutely no 'outbursts,' and I never got out of control. I should have taped those sessions. If you could hear a tape, I'm certain you would agree that at the most I might have shown a little frustration, which, by the way, was justified."

"And you are now in conflict with your chief psychiatrist, who, so far as you know, is fairly well liked by most of your associates, but has been abrasive in her communications with you?"

"Well, I don't know how many of the other docs like her. But I probably have a greater problem with her just because I'm so aboveboard and unwilling to cater to her need to flaunt her authority."

"Would you be willing to consider that you might be the one who needs to change?"

"Well, I might be able to learn some skills. There's no way I need psychotherapy. I thought you, as a psychologist, might be able to help me with some suggestions as to behavioral techniques for dealing with her authoritarian tactics. She acts like she thinks she's God!"

(This next suggestion from me pushed his buttons, and our conversation became difficult. I wasn't sure how to proceed, so I followed the time-honored advice given to counselors everywhere: "When you don't know what to say, tell the patient what you have heard him say." But, as you will observe, even this made him angry with me.)

"It really gets your goat to be pushed around, doesn't it, especially by a woman."

"Of course, I don't like being pushed around, Sherlock! And it has nothing to do with her being a woman—I am not prejudiced, like you're implying. She tries to tell me how to do things. Thinks she knows better how to medicate my patients than I do. The other day she told me I had given one guy enough Haldol to make him a zombie. My prescribed dose was perfectly reasonable. She takes advantage of her gender to lord it over me. *That's* what I don't like."

I ignored the slam and his assumption that I thought he had

something against women in general. He was right, that was my opinion. But I wanted to focus on what he really needed to do to make this relationship better. "Nobody likes being pushed around. It's stressful and hard on one's self-esteem."

"Yeah, I guess that's right."

"It hurts a man's pride to be told what to do by someone who might know less than him."

"Exactly. It amounts to an attack on my intelligence. Her superior attitude makes me mad. She tries to put me down. It is hard."

"I see what you mean. And you know, I agree with you that you don't have a psychological problem. I think it's a spiritual one. It's sin—a particular manifestation of the sinfulness we all have to battle. Yours is the deadly sin of pride. The mistaken idea that you can handle all this by changing someone else overlooks the fact that God wants you to handle your own pride by repentance—and by learning the habits of meekness, such as Jesus taught in His Beatitudes. For you, developing humility and meekness is the key to a life of abundant fulfillment instead of irritation, anger, and painful self-esteem problems."

"Hmm. I thought you were going to try to give me a diagnosis—some kind of paranoia or something. I never thought you would tell me I could be experiencing spiritual problems. I do believe in spiritual reality—I'm a Christian. As a psychiatrist, I'd rather have a colleague help me see my sin than to call me mentally ill."

I did have a series of sessions with Dr. Mortenson. Our conversations included prayer for conviction and repentance, a careful look at the example of Christ's humility in Philippians 2, and reduction of his anxiety over the possible loss of recognition, status, and acceptance. This anxiety had led to his fear of being dominated, humiliated, and practically vaporized by his professional superiors. Finally, we did some modeling and rehearsal of Christlike meekness in conversation and manner. As this man dropped his defensiveness, he found he did not need its "protection" and that his relationships with others based on his new openness and vulnerability became rewarding and enjoyable instead of threatening.

Battling Your Own Pride

Let me break down the process for fighting the deadly sin of pride into discreet steps. Like Dr. Mortenson, you will probably want to repeat this until you find yourself actually reducing the prevalence of proud behavior in your daily life:

1. *Pray for God's help and for the power of the Holy Spirit to change.* In battling sin, we are encouraged to depend on His sanctifying grace and motivation, as well as to realize that Christian believers can use their God-empowered will to take up the weapons of righteousness and choose to do right. Remember the three rules for success in chapter 1, restated below.

2. *Read the list of pride subtraits at the end of this chapter.* Determine the specific form(s) of your own pride. Is it controlling, presumptuous, status-seeking, attention-demanding, or something else? Perhaps you will decide to work on several manifestations. If so, it might be best to choose to work on one at a time.

3. *Apply the principle of consulting your internal speech.* Audit your thoughts. Form the habit of tuning in to what you are thinking, saying, and doing, paying special attention to thoughts generated by the devil, the world, or the flesh—manifestations of pride. Then pay attention to your own reborn spirit, your truth-instructed conscience. Discover within yourself a God-implanted desire to be a truly meek and humble person, talking to yourself with renewed humble thoughts.

4. *Apply the principle of choosing incompatible behavior.* This is a deliberate changing of your *self-talk* from proud misbeliefs to God-given truth and your *actions* from self-exalting behavior to Christlike behavior and the peace and joy it brings. It embraces three parts: (1) Confess your sin—be specific, detailed, and complete. You may confess to God in private or you may have a clergyperson or a Christian spouse, brother, or sister as one to whom you will be accountable;[5] (2) Believe (and remind yourself) that Jesus Christ died to take away the penalty and the

doing of this very sin—the act, the behavior, and the misbeliefs behind it—and that God is acting at this moment to forgive and empower you; and (3) Resolve, with the help of God, to stop doing the actions and maintaining the attitudes that constitute pride. Deliberately choose to do and say things that are incompatible with pride.

5. *Apply the principle of zealous determination. Energetically* determine not to allow pride to control you. *Enthusiastically* agree with Jesus' teaching in the Gospels and His examples of humility and service to others. Choose a way of serving someone else humbly and do it with all your heart.

Practice working with God's Spirit to change your thoughts and behavior, following these five steps throughout your study of the Seven Deadly Sins. Aim at change.

The Sin Test: Pride and Psychopathology

Through pride we sinners assert that *mine* is the kingdom and the power and the glory. This idea is reality distortion of the highest order. After searching for correlations between scores on the Sin Test and the diagnoses of psychiatric hospital patients, as well as correlations between Sin Test scores and MMPI scores, here is one of the findings: The psychiatric patients with the most prominent scores on the Pride Scale were those with more serious kinds of thinking disorders, including delusional beliefs, incompetent thinking, and poor reality testing. Those with schizophrenic and various brain syndrome diagnoses had significantly higher pride scores than other groups of psychiatric patients.

In other words, there *is* a connection between some kinds of pride and some kinds of reality distortion. Why? This intriguing result might be understood in terms of the proud person's severe dislocation of the center of his worldview. Whereas more humble people tend to see God (or other persons) as central, the proud person wants to see herself at the center. Every other ego, divine or human, is therefore a threat to her self-designated primacy. According to these findings, pride is not only sinful: It can become "sick," as well.

Pride in the Sin Test

Would you like to give yourself a brief pride quiz using some items from my experimental Sin Test? The following proved statistically to be some of the most powerful discriminators of pride. To try them yourself, answer each one True or False. There are no tricky items. "True" is always the direction indicative of pride. A single item does not necessarily point to an especially high pride score. The more items answered true, the more likely this is one of your deadly sin problems. (Incidentally, when you take the Sin Test in appendix 1, you will discover that the "sinful" direction of answers may be true or false, which is not the case in the brief quiz at the end of each chapter.)

_____ 1. There is no respect these days for people who really know what is going on.

_____ 2. A great many people have wrong ideas about religion simply because they are so limited and incapable of seeing things the way I do.

_____ 3. When I get into a conversation, I am uncomfortable unless I get people to talk about subjects I know a great deal about.

_____ 4. If other people fail to recognize how good I am, it is because of their own limitations.

_____ 5. I feel resentment when others fail to notice and praise me for my achievements.

_____ 6. I usually feel irritated when I have to take orders from others.

_____ 7. It is too bad the world has so many dull-witted, un-interesting people.

_____ 8. I have often had the thought that God plays around with people like puppets.

_____ 9. I often excuse my own mistakes as just due to "bad breaks," but when others make mistakes I tend to conclude that they just don't have what it takes to do things right.

_____ 10. What I do and think are none of God's business.

The following list contains a number of the subtraits of pride. Check those you believe apply to you or to the person you are evaluating:

_____ Insisting on autonomy: "I am in charge and I have every right to be in charge."

_____ Believing that "I know best: I am God—or else I ought to be God. I could do the job better than the Incumbent."

_____ Trying to be noticed

_____ Itching for compliments

_____ Hating being lowly and submissive

_____ Loathing to admit wrongdoing

_____ Being argumentative

_____ Refusing advice

_____ Acting defensively

_____ Being critical

_____ Being inconsiderate

_____ Being presumptuous

_____ Being boastful

_____ Being inordinately anxious about what others might think of you

_____ Being hypocritical

Examine Your Understanding of Pride

1. Pride is worse than merely thinking too highly of yourself. It is the unbridled conviction that you really ought to be . . .

2. Cassian taught that pride is the only sin that calls forth the opposition of . . .

3. What is wrong with the oft-heard mantra: "It's my life and I have a right to do as I choose"?

4. Milton, in *Paradise Lost,* told us that Satan thought he could . . .

5. Describe the prideful thinking of Raskolnikov in Dostoevsky's *Crime and Punishment.*

6. Nietzsche reasoned that if God is dead, then . . .

7. Explain what you understand to be "the pride of presumption."

For Further Thought and Discussion

1. Explain why you think anxiety might be caused by pride.

2. Do you usually admire proud people? Why? Or why not?

3. Do you think there is a difference between the deadly sin of pride and the pride referred to in the following: "What so proudly we hailed at the twilight's last gleaming . . ."; "I am very proud of my church for its willingness to help the poor"; "My children are my pride and joy!"; "Terry, clean your room! Have you no pride or self-respect?"

4. Can you figure out how every other sin springs from pride as its root? For example: Lying? Trying to act cool? Insulting someone? Doing a sloppy job at school or work; doing less than your best? Murder?

5. Do you think it's true that Jesus had more harsh words for the proud than for the people mired in sins of the flesh such as fornication or tax collecting? If so, why?

Notes

1. St. John Cassian, *The Twelve Books on the Institutes of the Coenobia*, book XII, chapter VII. Cited from the Internet.
2. John Milton, *Paradise Lost*, 1.34–43. Cited in Edward Weatherly, Harold Moffett, Charles Prouty, and Henry Noyes, *The English Heritage*, vol. 1 (Boston: Ginn and Co., 1945), 349.
3. Friedrich Nietzsche, *Thus Spake Zarathustra*, trans. Thomas Common (New York: The Modern Library, n.d.).
4. The *Minnesota Multiphasic Personality Inventory* (MMPI) has been the most used and most researched of all psychological tests over the past sixty years. Because of data from thousands of research studies, much is known about the meaning of MMPI profiles. The revised version, MMPI–2, is an update of the original inventory.
5. Although some readers will find it easy to think of confessing their sins to a human being who can mediate the gospel to them along with good counsel and gentle firmness, others will likely not even consider this an option. Whichever group you find yourself in, the first priority is to monitor your own behavior and bring it before God.

Chapter 3

Envy—The Sin That Promises Nothing Good

"Envy," wrote John of Damascus, "is sorrow in the face of your neighbor's good." Envy inflicts emotional pain on the sinner when a friend, a neighbor, a co-worker, a brother, or a sister gets something good that she doesn't have, especially if she perceives the beneficiary as her equal, peer, or—even worse—her inferior.

Envy is not jealousy. Although "jealousy" is often used as a synonym for envy, it is technically something else. While *envy* is illicit desire for the attributes or possessions of another, *jealousy* is the desire to keep what is your own. This is not necessarily sinful; God is jealous, but He is never envious.

Strictly speaking, jealousy is fear of losing something, vigilance in guarding what is already yours. In some contexts it is far from being wrong, and indeed it may be quite appropriate. The Lord calls himself "a jealous God" (Exodus 20:5). A woman who is jealous of her spouse, for example, would be appropriately vexed if he were to flirt with someone else.

An audience can be brought to tears by Othello's tormented *jealousy* over his lovely and innocent bride, Desdemona, but the same crowd would feel only contempt for Saul's *envious* hurling

of a javelin at young David (1 Samuel 18). Saul, the first king
of Israel, is the great scriptural example of murderous envy.

> As they were coming home, when David returned from
> slaying the Philistine, the women came out of all the cities
> of Israel, singing and dancing, to meet King Saul, with tim-
> brels, with songs of joy, and with instruments of music. And
> the women sang to one another as they made merry, "Saul
> has slain his thousands, and David his ten thousands." And
> Saul was very angry, and this saying displeased him; he said,
> "They have ascribed to David ten thousands, and to me
> they have ascribed thousands; and what more can he have
> but the kingdom?" And Saul eyed David from that day on
> (vv. 6–9).

What a day! What a victory! Thanks be to God, the army of
Israel, which had been within a hairbreadth of defeat for lack of
courage, was *not* marching home in disgrace and dishonor. Because of the valor of the youngest son of Jesse, none would declare the men of Saul fainthearted cowards. David had brought
down the giant with his shepherd's sling and a single smooth
stone, and Israel's army gained a never-to-be-forgotten victory.
The Philistine troops turned tail and fled in terror, demoralized
by the loss of their champion to a mere boy. Saul's troops, now
energized, gave hot pursuit and decimated the enemy ranks. So
as they returned in triumph, the populace thronged to greet
them, acclaiming the mettle and pluck of their heroes. Saul delighted in the smiling eyes and victory songs of the women who
had turned out to greet the returning soldiers.

But what was this they were chanting? Saul's high spirits
crashed and his benign smile turned to fury. The louts were ap-
plauding not King Saul, the commander-in-chief, but the strip-
ling David. This mere boy was getting the glory due the king!
After this event, Saul's paranoid envy never abated but burned
in his heart until one day, while David played soothing melodies
for his healing, it burst into flame, and Saul suddenly hurled a
spear intending to pin David to the wall. He missed.

The Sin That Promises Nothing Good

Envy, like all the other sins, is a child of pride. As Thomas Aquinas quotes St. Gregory: "When the queen of vices, pride, has fully overcome and captured a heart, she presently hands it over to be laid waste by her generals, the seven principal vices [of which pride is also one], whence multitudes of other vices have their origin."[1] If *pride* is the sin of reality distortion to the point where a person persuades himself that he is supreme, *envy* is the result when reality lashes back to shatter his proud delusion. In other words, at just the moment when you are feeling splendid about your own importance, telling yourself how very good you are, someone or something appears to eclipse your imagined brilliance. Outstripped, outdone, overtaken, you can only chew the bitter pill and nurse your anguish.

When you are in thrall to this deadly sin, you suffer pungent pain. Of all the vices, envy may be the most agonizing for sinners. One often overlooked characteristic of sin is this: *Most* sins promise a pleasurable or profitable result—"Just do it and you will enjoy a quick reward." This guarantee isn't always false, for often a reward *is* attached—either a positive benefit or an escape from something painful. You may actually get what you were promised. At first.

This was the case, for instance, with the original sin. Adam and Eve were told that they need only taste a delicious morsel from the tree of knowledge to gain a splendid benefit: They would become wise. What could be better? Wise in the "knowledge of good and evil"—that certainly sounded desirable. Well, they did obtain it: Experiential knowledge of evil was added to their previous enjoyment of perfect good. Their pride fulfilled its promise.

Most sins offer something you think you want, and they may perform as advertised, delivering the predicted slick results—for a while. Pride offers the euphoria of preeminence, anger promises the joy of revenge, greed promises the security of abundant wealth, sloth promises welcome release from the chains of effort, lust promises the thrill of nerve-ending sensations, and gluttony promises pleasures galore. But envy—it is the exception. Of all the vices, only envy never promises or delivers anything but bitterness and misery.

Nobody sings envy's praises. There will be no *North American Society for the Promotion of Envy*. There is no annual *Begrudgers' Pride Parade*. Nothing on *The Art of Envy* has made it into even the most avant-garde school curriculum. Do you sit around wishing you could find more time for envying? An absurd question! Do you yearn to envy your friend for his new car? Do you drool for the right to envy someone their IQ, their income, their gorgeous home, their spirituality, their answers to prayer, their amazing children, or anything else?

God will not interfere with your spite. But there is no way you would *willingly* choose such vexation. As Angus Wilson put it, "Envy is impotent, numbed with fear, yet never ceasing in its appetite; and it knows no gratification save endless self-torment."[2]

A shocking fable from Aesop bludgeons this lesson home. It seems that two neighbors came before Zeus and begged him to grant their hearts' desire. Now, the one was full of greed, and the other eaten up with envy. Therefore, to punish them both, Zeus granted that each might have whatever he wished for himself, but only on condition that his neighbor had twice as much.

The greedy man prayed to have a roomful of gold. No sooner said than done; but all his joy was turned to grief when he found that his neighbor had two rooms full of the precious metal. Then came the turn of the envious man who could not bear to think that his neighbor had any joy at all. So he prayed that he might have one of his own eyes put out, by which means his companion would become totally blind.[3]

A Case of Envy

Let me describe for you an example of envy appearing in my clinical case load. Marie was an attractive young mother of two who turned out to be a difficult client. For months, she told me, a close friend had been urging her to "get some help!"

Marie had worn out her husband, Bernie, by harping on her preoccupation.

She appeared for her initial interview neatly (even stunningly) dressed, bantered with the receptionist, poured a cup of coffee, and acted as though she were a guest at a party. In the consulting room, she smiled pleasantly and asked after my health. "I'm fine, thanks," I replied, "and ready to hear a little about you. I'm curious as to what brings you to see me today."

"I'm embarrassed, and I probably shouldn't have come. It's just silly. I'm afraid you'll think I'm wasting your time—or tell me I'm losing my mind. It's so ridiculous. But I can't help it." Her eyes moistened and she daubed a bit with her handkerchief. She smiled again; I waited. "I thought I would get over this myself, but it doesn't get better."

When a client begins her first session like this, it often reveals a terrible fear of being ridiculed. She tries to preclude my telling her she is being foolish and silly for even consulting a psychologist by preempting that line and labeling herself silly first. From her appearance and style, I found it hard to believe she was a tormented soul. Her complaint was anxiety, but the symptoms she described were the kind presented by people who are depressed: sleep and appetite difficulties and feelings of sadness and regret that wouldn't go away.

"Why don't you tell me what you're anxious about?" I suggested.

"Okay, it's about my house. My husband and I designed our new home. We moved in six months ago. It was just fine until we went to that party at the Bentleys'. I fell hopelessly in love with their house and now I can't stand ours!" Marie habitually ratcheted up her feelings to the tenth power for emphasis, but this time her distress was genuine and severe.

"But your house is brand-new. You just built it—designed it exactly the way you wanted it," I replied.

"I know. But when I saw what the Bentleys had done with their four-season porch, I realized ours should have been built exactly like it. And I haven't been able to get over it. I wish I had their house instead of mine." Her soliloquies were punctuated by sighs and tears. "I hate my house," she kept saying.

Marie could hardly get her mind off the belief that her family's new home was an awful mistake. "I tell myself over and over again that this is ridiculous. I should just get over it. I should get my mind on something else. But I can't stop thinking about it. And I've been crying a lot lately." She was certainly obsessed with her misery.

After a few sessions, it was obvious we were getting nowhere—I wasn't even sure what to call the problem. We had been trying to discover her anxiety misbeliefs and fearful self-talk, but there was no improvement. Marie's physician had prescribed Serzone, but although this drug is an effective anti-depressant and a fairly good treatment for obsessions, she had gotten absolutely no relief. She went along with what I was doing, but she lacked the upbeat reactions and expressions of those who sense that they have found the key to their troubles and believe they would be able to use it to get better. She also didn't exhibit the exhilaration clients often display when they discover how misbeliefs and self-talk elicit their depression. We puzzled together about this lack of change.

Almost every counselor asks a fundamental, integral question early on; for some reason, I had so far failed to do so, perhaps taking for granted that she had explored it with previous therapists. I asked it now: "Has this sort of thing happened before? You took an important step when you decided to come in for help, because the problem is not your house, and you showed you understand that by seeing me. My guess is that this problem is an old habit. I don't know how old, but perhaps you can think back to the earliest point in life you can remember having these or similar feelings. Our time is up for today, but it would be useful if you could work on this a little by yourself. See what you can remember and how far back you can recall."

At our next interview, she could hardly wait to tell me what she had done. "I actually got in the car and went to _____ (the small town where she had grown up). And when I crossed the railroad tracks, all sorts of memories returned along with old, sad feelings. We lived on the 'wrong side' of the tracks. My family was so poor we kids had to wear hand-me-downs and makeshifts while the other kids came to school each year in new outfits. We never had new toys, only stuff from the thrift shop; we wore mittens with holes in them, socks too. We were heckled and teased. I always acted as if the bullies didn't bother me, and I tried not to cry until I could get away by myself, but I came to the conclusion that we were poor because we were worthless and unimportant. The other kids had good things, but everything we had was junk. So I thought that meant we were junk too."

As Marie painted a picture of a childhood in poverty, I felt sorrow in my own heart, sympathizing with her dejection and hopelessness, the sense of insignificance and inferiority she must have experienced. I asked myself why being poor had affected her as it did. After all, poverty was widespread during the Great Depression years when I grew up, but my friends and I never thought of ourselves as inferior because of it. What was different for Marie? The answer was plain: being different. The poverty of *her* family was different; the other kids were not poor. It was during those years that she had developed the tendency of comparing herself and whatever she had with others and what they had, and she had also formed the habit—this is important—of concluding that whatever others had was better. And that meant that everybody else was better as well.

All her life Marie had been practicing two habits, joined together at the hip: compare and conclude. She routinely, almost automatically, compared herself and her assets with other people and theirs. Then, again by default, she concluded that what others had was better. We gathered enough examples from her stored memories to be certain: She was miserable all right, but not from a mental illness, or at least that wasn't her primary problem. It was the deadly sin of *envy*.

But how was I going to tell her? Some clients should not be informed as to their diagnosis; these are people who might readily yet wrongly twist a clinical label into a message of hopelessness. And people go to psychologists to learn how to recover from neurosis, not to be told they are sinners. On the other hand, most clients come to see me precisely because they want to talk with a Christian psychologist about truth. For some, the discovery that their problem is sin would be meaningful and helpful—even a relief. They know that God has provided a great remedy for sin in Jesus Christ, that the outlook for sinners is hopeful, and that His truth is good news. In other words, I was fairly certain Marie would not be stunned if I mentioned sin. I decided to find out.

"Marie, would you be willing to explore the possibility that some of the trouble here might be caused by sin?"

"Sin? Well, that's something I hadn't thought of. But—I suppose I would. In fact, you've piqued my interest. What do you mean?"

"I mean that the habit pattern you've described sounds exactly like the sin of envy—feeling bad over the good things someone else receives and degrading your own things by comparison. You've told me that this is precisely what is hurting you, or more accurately, this is how you're hurting yourself. Whenever you decide that someone else has it better than you, all hell breaks loose (literally). The deadly sin of envy is not just no fun; it's pure torture!"

"This does seem like what's bothering me. I've been getting upset over comparing our house with the Bentleys'—and this is a lifelong habit. But where does that get us? The thing is still there, and I haven't been able to get rid of it."

"That's the point. If this is the deadly sin of envy, and I believe it is, you might be able to break the *habit* by yourself or with the help of a behavioral psychologist, but the *sinful root* cannot be cured by you or by me. *God* has a real cure for sin: Jesus Christ. I know you have committed your life to Him and that you can enlist the aid of His Holy Spirit in breaking the powerful grip of this sin habit along with its roots."

Not a Mere Quirk—A Deadly Sin

You can see from what I have already told you that Marie's problem was not merely a psychological anomaly or an emotional illness but the lethal sin of envy. I helped her to recognize not only the sin problem but also a specific remedy she could apply. The truth was good news to her!

Here, in a nutshell, is what Marie did to develop a new, healing behavioral sequence: Whenever she felt the old pain, she used it as a reminder to check her self-talk and to isolate the envious "comparing and concluding" that generated miserable emotions.[4] Using her will, she chose to tell herself she had the power to generously rejoice at God's good gifts to others, to sincerely will their good *even if it appeared to be better than the good gifts of God to her.* Her qualities and abilities came from God; they had to be good *even at those times when they amounted to obstacles or corrections,* because God would always give her precisely what she needed, just as He has given others precisely what He knows they need.

From that point on, Marie began to receive the good even out of troubles and difficulties. She kept reporting definite improvement in her sense of well-being. At first, the idea of using her will to apply her faith to her self-talk was new. She had been a rather casual Christian; now she did some serious repenting and praying for faith. It had never occurred to her that she could use her will to make choices. But soon she gave up smoking cigarettes, a change she had despaired of *ever* managing to accomplish. She countered her envy with acts of service and generosity. She "went on her way rejoicing," and before long her anxiety and depression were diminished to the point where we saw no reason to continue our counseling sessions. Often, simply putting a label on a sin or an illness—calling it what it is—allows healing to begin. Coming face-to-face with stark reality can be a first step toward overcoming the problem.

Envy and Sibling Rivalry

Where did we learn how to envy? Does everyone acquire the sinful habits of comparing and concluding during childhood, as Marie did? That is, do most people begin to envy others at the stage of sibling rivalry? So far as I can determine, the concept of sibling rivalry was *developed* by Sigmund Freud (1856–1939), but he didn't *invent* the phenomenon—in Bible history, the first murder was motivated by sibling rivalry.

Regardless of who coined the term, the idea is right on the money. Sibling rivalry, say psychologists, occurs in most families: Siblings compete with one another for parental attention, praise, and favors. If you are a parent of more than one child, you have surely heard the complaints: "How come *he* gets to go and *I* don't?" or "You *always* stick up for her!" No matter how sensible they seem to you, distinctions you make between your children's privileges will not appear logical to them. Why do your attempts to explain that "she can have this because she is older than you" or "he can do that because he earned it" fail? The pouting complainer continues to believe you are unfair, and sibling rivalry often carries over into adult life. I have seen grown men who struggle with their siblings for parental approval until the day their parents die.

And what is sibling rivalry but envy? Ordinary people like you and me can suffer awful pangs because of it. Some of us are consumed with worry and frustration because our closest friends can afford a world tour; our neighbor's child won a scholarship to an Ivy League school; the person next door drives a Deville ("How in heaven's name can she afford such an expensive car?"); Harold, that ridiculous clown, gets all the attention at parties; Gina talks endlessly about her spiritual gifts, and you're sick of listening. A co-worker gets the promotion you deserved, so you tell yourself it doesn't pay to be smart and to work hard. He sings better than you do; she has nicer hair; he gets to travel a lot; she seems to be very close to the pastor; he speaks up in class and talks at great length, while the teacher cuts you off if you try to say anything; she has a better husband; he has a sexier wife. Amy gets a place in the dance competition, and you're cut; he has charm, she has good looks; they have scintillating conversations, we never talk to each other. Even the other person's virtues or integrity or spiritual progress may appear unfair because they seem so far ahead of your own.

The Lonely Crowd

I say "may appear unfair" because our envy is often based on our own *imagined inferiority* or *fancied mistreatment*. That is, we may *believe* George has everything, when, if George were to tell you what is on his heart, he would surprise you. It may be that he longs for what you have instead of contenting himself with what is his own. David Riesman, author of *The Lonely Crowd*, maintains that our culture has produced what he calls "other-directed" people. Rather than basing our behavior on internalized standards, he suggests, we "other-directeds" derive our rules from imitating what others do, say, and think. Writing in the 1950s, Riesman describes his society as one where nearly everybody is perpetually scanning what others think, what others do, and what others have. The other-directed man or woman is always anxiously comparing, comparing, comparing.

For other-directed people, envy is *a way of life*. They frequently *imagine* their friends delighting in exciting recreation, interesting travel, and thrilling sex lives, while their own experiences are dull and drab by comparison. That was then—the palmy days of the '50s. Then came the '60s, where arrogance and pride took charge and produced full-blown cultural revolt. Rebellion by the young was the latest approved fad—from Jerry Rubin's literary disgrace entitled *Steal This Book* to the silly spectacle of students being allowed to "occupy" university presidents' offices and to present their "demands," and the even more ludicrous curiosity of those in authority bowing to the mandates of eighteen-year-old children! The youth were teaching us all, bringing us into the Age of Aquarius; we were all enjoined to love one another and share alike.

At first glance, it appeared that the "young idealists" brought up by Riesman's lonely crowd had abandoned envy in favor of arrogant pride. Well, maybe. Until we remember the complaining by those flower children about the rich and what the rich had and did. Until we remember the resentment of those who couldn't stand to think of Honeywell making all that money building big bad bombs—more money than us, that's for sure. Or the wealthy owners of evil businesses like forestry and the production of petroleum products. The trees, we were told, ought to belong to all of us, and oil should be left in the earth, which is the mother of us all. Do you see how envy of the rich and the powerful might have been masked as phony crusades? Many of the so-called demands for "social justice" were often no more than demonstrations of pure envy.

Does Riesman's "other-directedness" explain envy? Not really. Not its radical cause, at least. Sociologists, psychoanalysts, and psychologists may describe some things about *behavior*, but for a truly powerful explanation of such self-generated wretchedness—sin—as envy, we need to turn to God's revelation.

> Wherefore, as by one man sin entered into the world, and death by sin; and so death passed upon all men, for that all have sinned (Romans 5:12 KJV).
>
> If we say that we have no sin, we deceive ourselves, and the truth is not in us. . . . If we say that we have not sinned, we make him a liar, and his word is not in us (1 John 1:8, 10 KJV).

God alone knows the deep underground springs from which our envy bubbles to the surface; therefore, His Word alone reveals the true source of envy and all other sins. Models, influences, and conditioning from our experiences may fashion the specific shapes of our choices, thoughts, and actions. But the inclination to do evil starts at birth—we are born with hearts bent toward sin. As we examine the symptoms of this deadly sin, we need to realize that since no human being has a perfect heart—all of us have remnants of the sinful old self still with us—we will probably see ourselves in some or all of the envy symptoms mentioned here. For some of us this sin will be more dominating than for others, and for some it may amount to only a faint whisper within. Whatever the case may be it is important for us to notice our own envy and work toward its elimination.

Detecting Envy

You *can* perceive envy in yourself and others, and here are some signs: Envy shows itself when we engage in "sour grapes" talk, putting down those we envy most and placing the worst possible construction on their actions. Maybe your critical friend who regularly issues negative judgments becomes even more critical when you have praised or commended someone else. Or maybe *you* are the critical one. This is a behavioral indication of the disorder of envy.

Another sign of envy can be exceptional competitiveness. Not every desire to play games and sports springs from wickedness (as some would have us believe), nor should all striving for excellence be chalked up to envy. But when the real goal is not the simple pleasure of athletics or earning a living playing football, when it is not excellence in service to God and man but only the grotesque, insidious satisfaction of beating up someone else, we are indulging sinful envy. This sin trait may goad an envious person to embrace ambitious effort and rock-hard determination to *surpass* those he or she envies. And it may even lead to worldly achievement, success, and acclaim.

But the price of envy-driven accomplishments is terribly high: a life with little or no peace and joy. For the envious, such successes, like the conquests of a Don Juan, fail to satisfy. The instant something he has struggled to attain becomes his, he begins to disparage it in favor of something else that belongs to his neighbor. Whatever is yours seems somehow tawdry in comparison with the glittering attributes and flashy toys of others. For the envious, coming into possession of something makes it suddenly worthless *because and only because* it is yours and not someone else's. Could this phenomenon have something to do with low self-esteem? And could the self-disparagement of the envious person so resemble genuine humility that we may confuse the two? For example, an extremely proud person might appear humble simply because envy causes him to bad-mouth himself, as well as whatever or whomever belongs to him.

Do you sometimes notice that you dislike another person

and have trouble finding a good reason for it? Could this person be an object of your envy? One whose envy is extreme ends up as a tightly wound ball of hatred, loathing all those she imagines better or more fortunate than she. Even the "good loser" syndrome, says Angus Wilson, with its "strange hearty tones that somehow come out as a snarl . . . or a snakelike hiss" may emerge as nothing more than a thin and unsuccessful mask over the face of envy.[5]

This disposition, as described, is clearly painful and undesirable, as well as maladaptive. Nevertheless, the Bible and classical theologians have insisted that envy is not a misunderstanding, not a mistake, not a victimization, not an illness, but a *sin* in the same sense in which pride is a sin: Like pride, envy is rebellion against God. Jesus himself establishes it as sin rather than an environmental or social defect:

> And Jesus said, "What comes out of a man is what defiles a man. For from within, out of the heart of man, come evil thoughts, fornication, theft, murder, adultery, coveting, wickedness, deceit, licentiousness, envy, slander, pride, foolishness. All these evil things come from within, and they defile a man" (Mark 7:20–23).

What is sinful about envy? *Envy is directly opposed to God's will that His children love one another.* Love requires a person to rejoice in another's good (1 Corinthians 13:6); envy requires him to mourn over it.

A Species of Depression?

Among the results of my Sin-Test experiment, envy was significantly correlated with depression, the kind of sadness that is negative, bitter, tense, and guilty. Most clinicians will likely fail to think of sin as a cause of such wretchedness, but envy ought to be considered sinful and thus treated with the healing power of Christ Jesus. Please note: Although envy can cause depression, not all depression is caused by envy. Other sins, as well as non-sinful factors like neurotransmitter* problems, apparently can cause this serious emotional disorder. Shall I repeat this so that no reader will run around labeling all depressed people envious?

By the way, antidepressant medications such as Prozac cause improvement in 60 to 70 percent of depressed persons. Could it be that these medications are effective in people who are depressed for reasons other than envy? Perhaps envy depression does not respond to medication. Sounds like an experiment waiting to be performed!

As does the proud, the envious character often has a self-worth problem; he goes around arguing the case for and against his own significance or value. But here the only admissible evidence consists of signals from the *external, temporal, this-worldly environment,* specifically in the performance, possessions, achievements, and qualities of others that must be constantly compared with his own. As soon as any comparison with friends or peers is unfavorable, the envious character experiences great pain.

What Can Be Done?

It is likely that some of us have been thinking, "I certainly experience the pangs of envy, but as far as I can see, I don't *choose* to envy. It's just something I feel." And you're right: Envy is in the roots of the old sinful flesh, and resolve cannot heal it. The healing of envy must be *spiritual;* that is, healing for sin cannot succeed except by the work of the Holy Spirit in the believer. The only foundation for an individual's significance or value must be found in what cannot be altered by ever-changing circumstances, such as those the envious use to measure their worth. Eventually, every circumstantial gauge will read "low" or "empty altogether." The true basis for cure is the kindness of the Lord that we encounter in the Word.

---

*Neurotransmitters are brain chemicals that facilitate the proper functioning of nerve cells.

> So put away all malice and all guile and insincerity and
> envy and all slander. Like newborn babes, long for the pure
> spiritual milk, that by it you may grow up to salvation; for
> you have tasted the kindness of the Lord (1 Peter 2:1–3).

Christ is the cure because He is like a tunnel through all the
debris piled up by the world, a tunnel through to the other side,
the eternal side (this is what eternal life means). There a brand-
new discovery awaits—the discovery of who one is in God, an-
chored in God, planted in God, built on the firm foundation of
God, standing sure because "the Lord knows those who are
His" (2 Timothy 2:19).

If you need to work at breaking the power of your envy, if
this is a troublesome deadly sin of yours, you must start at the
beginning. Bring it to the cross by confessing it to God and perhaps also to a pastor or a fellow believer who knows what to do
with confession of sin. Ask God's forgiveness and make a promise to resist the untruthful thoughts and actions of envy in yourself from here on.

Can you do anything else? Yes. Remember the value of the
principle of incompatible behavior? It states that if you are busy
doing one thing, you cannot be doing another thing that's incompatible with it. For instance, if you are at the moment ex-
ploding in fury at someone, you cannot at the same time be
paralyzed with fear and anxiety. *What the Scriptures teach us to
be and do is incompatible with envy.* This is living by the Spirit
through Christ Jesus.

> But the fruit of the Spirit is love, joy, peace, patience,
> kindness, goodness, faithfulness, gentleness, self-control;
> against such there is no law. And those who belong to Christ
> Jesus have crucified the flesh with its passions and desires.
> If we live by the Spirit, let us also walk by the Spirit. Let us
> have no self-conceit, no provoking of one another, no envy
> of one another (Galatians 5:22–26).

Pray for the Holy Spirit of truth to help you tell yourself the
truth in place of the glaring misbeliefs that kindle the fires of
envy. You must use your regenerated will to practice kindness,

love, even generosity. *Love and envy are incompatible.* We cannot deeply love and at the same time envy, for in love we wish the very best for others. If you cannot directly choose your own feelings, you can choose two other things: (1) what you tell yourself; and (2) what you do.

First, by the empowerment of the Holy Spirit, take up the weapons of truth with which to battle your lying, envious misbeliefs. Journal them as they come up so you can clearly identify them as envy, and then replace them with pure, clear, truthful thoughts of generosity and charity. You may be struggling with, "How awful it is that she has *X, Y,* or *Z* when I deserve it as much or more." Instead, learn to see and speak the truth to yourself: "I cannot know that person as God does, and if her gifts are good and perfect, they are from God, who never makes a mistake. I can decide that I believe God's will is best, and I can rest in the confidence that God knows what He's doing rather than making myself tense and telling Him what to do."

Second, as I work on my misbeliefs, I can also change my actions. I can pray for the person I envy. I can refuse to try to beat and better and outdo him. I can practice more generous giving to aid others in need. I can cultivate what God has given me. The development and deployment of my own gifts and possessions for the practice of kindness and love can take up all my efforts so that I have no time to envy my neighbor.

You might find it helpful to memorize Ecclesiastes 4:4: "Then I saw that all toil and all skill in work come from a man's envy of his neighbor. This also is vanity and a striving after wind."

Envy in the Sin Test

Would you like to give yourself a brief envy quiz? The following items proved statistically to be some of the most powerful envy discriminators in my experiments with the Sin Test. To try them yourself, answer each one True or False.

_F_   1. If I hear an associate faulted for a drastic mistake who was consistently getting more credit than I, it would make me feel better.

_F_   2. I must admit that I enjoy conversations in which the faults or misdeeds of others are being discussed.

_F_   3. I like to be around people who are less gifted than I.

_F_   4. It would give me pleasure to be at a party where someone more popular than I am suffered extreme embarrassment.

_F_   5. Very virtuous people irritate me.

_T_   6. I secretly feel good when I learn that someone I dislike has gotten into trouble.

_F_   7. Sometimes when others speak too highly of an acquaintance, I try to point this out.

_T_   8. Even though I know it's not right, I can't help feeling a little enjoyment when someone at the top of the heap takes a tumble.

_F_   9. I get distressed when one of my friends surpasses me in a field where I have worked hard to become competent.

_F_   10. I would never take as much pleasure from a friend's success as I would if it were my own.

Every "true" response is an envy indicator. All people are sinners and will probably have some "true" responses. The principle behind the Sin Test is not discovering whether or not we have sins, but rather discovering where we especially need to pray and work in the battle against sin.

Examine Your Understanding of Envy

1. John of Damascus defined envy as "sorrow in the face of your _____."

2. Jealousy is/is not exactly the same as envy (circle the correct choice).

3. Envy can be elicited by the spiritual _____ of someone else.

4. David Riesman, author of *The Lonely Crowd,* saw a good deal of envy motivating the people of the 1950s. He used the term _____-_____ to describe this characteristic.

6. An envious person may desire something very much, but the moment he owns the thing, it becomes _____ in his eyes.

7. The opposite of envy is _____ (1 Corinthians 13:6).

For Further Thought and Discussion

---

1. The moral theologians have usually concluded that all the Seven Deadly Sins are outgrowths of pride. How do you think envy is connected with pride?

2. A puzzling question: Why do we envy anyone for anything, since envy never promises us a reward? In other words, since envy has no allure and is nothing but misery, why do we envy?

3. Some people believe that playing competitive games is harmful to the less-skilled players. Do you think all competitive sports and competitive games must provoke envy in the participants?

4. How is the sin of envy linked to feelings of depression?

Notes

1. *Basic Writings of Saint Thomas Aquinas*, Vols. I & II, Anton C. Pegis, ed. (New York: Random House, 1945), Moral XXXI.
2. Angus Wilson, et al., *The Seven Deadly Sins* (New York: William Morrow, 1962), 11.
3. *Aesop's Fables*, trans. George Fyler Townsend. http://classics.mit.edu/Aesop/fab.html.
4. A much more thorough discussion of truth therapy methods and how to apply them can be found in my book *Learning to Tell Myself the Truth*. This book takes the reader through a six-week program for accomplishing emotional change through truth.
5. Wilson, 4–5.

Chapter 4

Anger—Wrong or Right? When and How?

Like many people, Nathan came to consult me because his rampant, overpowering anger was destroying his life. Yet he was convinced that other people and their unfair treatment created his difficulties, and he was determined not to consider his own habitual wrath. We will take an up-close look at Nathan and his complaints later. But first, we need to look at our own confusion.

For people at one extreme, anger is the ultimate virtue—provided that you aim your anger at *their* approved targets. There are also some who have interesting ideas as to anger's role in our existence; a movie producer, apparently believing anger would fit nicely into the devotional life, called his debut film *Praying with Anger*.[1] *Is* anger acceptable, so long as I have a good reason to be mad? Is it really just "gland secretion," as Stanley J. Sharpless puts it? (See this book's opening poem.) Is anger, as some say, perfectly normal, not sinful at all, unless you harm someone?

At the *opposite* extreme are those who agree with the stringent view of St. John Cassian—that anger is (practically always) a dangerous deadly sin:

The athlete of Christ who strives lawfully ought thoroughly to root out the feeling of wrath. And it will be a sure remedy for this disease, if in the first place we make up our mind that we ought never to be angry at all, whether for good or bad reasons: as we know that we shall at once lose the light of discernment, and the security of good counsel, and our very uprightness, and the temperate character of righteousness, if the main light of our heart has been darkened by its shadows: next, that the purity of our soul will presently be clouded, and that it cannot possibly be made a temple for the Holy Ghost while the spirit of anger resides in us; lastly, that we should consider that we ought never to pray, nor pour out our prayer to God, while we are angry.[2]

A Serious Problem and a Deadly Sin

It seems to me Cassian's notion that followers of Christ Jesus ought *never* to be angry at all conflicts with Jesus' own teaching and example. But whatever we may think of Cassian's argument, one thing is sure: He did not take the matter of anger lightly. Do you? I admit that, for me, the crucial importance of the issue has increased greatly over the past ten years or so. It's obvious to me that while some anger is approved by God, Scripture is cautious about endorsing it. I think I have frequently been too generous. The approved category now appears much smaller than I had thought, while the unapproved category is stuffed with most of the everyday "angry episodes" to which we sinners are prone. It is these peeved moments, nursed grudges, and irritated outbursts that we, along with our counselors, too freely and too regularly justify.

Matthew, Mark, Luke, and John did not record the Gospels as biographies, so most of the life of Jesus on earth is not known to us (see, for example, John 21:25). Even so, perhaps the distance between Cassian's argument and Jesus' example isn't so great. As far as I know, all of Jesus' recorded history recounts only *three* episodes of His anger. These are described in John 2:13–17; Matthew 21:12; and Mark 3:5.

Some instances of anger even clearly equate with murder. As

this is being written, a news item tells the sickening story of a child's mother's lover, annoyed beyond endurance and unaccustomed to controlling his own emotions, battering the life out of a screaming infant. Sadly, this is not even an isolated, rare occurrence. "Straight out of hell," say most folks. Nobody hesitates to identify such destructive acts of raging violence.

A Chilling Tale of Fury

An even more hair-raising tale was told by the Greek playwright Euripides (fifth century B.C.) in his tragic play *Medea*. I once saw the great Dame Judith Anderson in the title role of this unforgettable drama of gut-wrenching anger in which Medea, the wife of unfaithful Jason (of the Golden Fleece), takes vengeance on his adultery by strangling their two dear little boys. Euripides' skill in evoking in the audience at once the sensation of Medea's mother-love at war against her towering rage, and at the same time their own mounting terror at the grisly scene they know is coming, is perhaps unmatched in all literature. For most people, denouncing Medea's response to her anger is a piece of cake.

Anger's Good Use

But discerning and reacting to anger is seldom so uncomplicated. Much angry behavior involves no violence, no rage, no verbal putdowns—only moderate and occasionally even constructive expressions. And most episodes of our *own* wrath seem to us reasonable; it's hard to be objective in the heat of our personal exasperation. Yet according to John Cassian, there is only one good use for anger:

> We have . . . a use for anger . . . for which alone it is . . . profitable for us, viz., when we are indignant and [we] rage against the lustful emotions of our heart, and are vexed at the things which we are ashamed to do or say.[3]

"Go ahead and be angry," says Cassian, "at your own sinful

nature! Nothing else." Martin Luther, somewhat less exacting, recognized that there are a few occasions when it may be right for believers to become angry at another person. But he also insisted that such occasions are rare.

The Bible: Is Anger Always Wrong, Never Wrong, or What?

Of all the moral theologians I have read, only John Cassian held the view that anger is *always* wrong. All the others have emphasized that (1) biblical teaching about anger never encourages us to simply "let it all hang out," and that (2) it nevertheless *is* possible to be angry without sin.

Let me summarize the relevant New Testament passages: Mark 3:5 ascribes the emotion of anger to Jesus; Mark 11:15 depicts His angry actions against the moneygrubbers in God's own house; Ephesians 4:26–27 stops short of condemning anger but insists that it be dealt with, not left to fester: "Be angry but do not sin; do not let the sun go down on your anger, and give no opportunity to the devil."

James 1:19 counsels a "look before you leap" policy: "Be slow to anger." This and the previous three references are sometimes cited to prove that blanket condemnation of all anger goes too far. But we must not rush to the other extreme. James informs us (right after the words "Be slow to anger"), that "the anger of man does not work the righteousness of God." There are five additional references in which Jesus and the apostolic writers include anger in the lists of sinful behavior to be purged out of the Christian's repertoire: 2 Corinthians 12:20; Galatians 5:20; Ephesians 4:31; Colossians 3:8; and 1 Timothy 2:8.

The teachings of Scripture and most moral theologians agree on this: Yes, it *may* happen that a righteous person becomes appropriately furious for good cause. But *pure righteous anger is rare.* Our problem is the tendency each of us has to believe that "in my case uprightness is the rule, not the exception"; we think our own anger must be right because it is ours. How do we manage this? By indulging in a widespread but erroneous belief: "Since I feel so upset, I must have been unfairly injured. Therefore, my angry reaction is righteous." In other words, "Because I'm so mad, you must have done something bad."

This is a fallacious argument, based not on the facts of the case but on the *intensity of our feelings*. The Bible (and theologians who are careful to follow biblical guidance) will not help us much in justifying our anger unless it happens to be (1) directed at our own sinful flesh; or (2) meekly accompanied with sorrowful concern for the evildoer with whom we may be forced to deal. The great teachers who have written about the deadly sin of anger know from personal experience how easily we are blinded and made incapable of discerning the truth about our own behavior.

When Anger Is Nothing but Emotion

So anger is a deadly sin? Well, yes. But, contrary to John Cassian, not always. While pride and envy, greed and gluttony, sloth and lust are *always* contrary to God's will for us, anger isn't—even if we have such difficulty being honest about our own wrath. Most classical theologians have concluded that in some instances, a person may innocently experience anger as nothing more than a natural response to an injury. The emotion of anger consists of sympathetic nervous system arousal including increased heart rate, raised blood pressure, dilation of capillaries, tensing of muscles, dilation of ocular pupils, and so forth. These are the basic provisions of the Creator for the occasion when it might be necessary to ward off an aggressor in self-defense, and this is why all these physiological fireworks have been called the "fight or flight response."

When Anger Is Just, Temperate, and Loving

Some people (erroneously) condemn certain emotions as evil, but an emotion cannot be considered sinful in itself. Our emotions are given to us by our Designer, so they are as morally neutral as our eyes or hands. Moreover, say nearly all moral teachers, God has not forbidden even certain punitive actions, provided these actions are *just, temperate, and loving.* Some of us have been taught that whatever we think or say, however insulting or humiliating, is permissible as long as we refrain from physical aggression. And it is true, for the most part, that you can't be arrested for your thoughts, feelings, and words—this comes close to the *legal* criterion. But it is far from the *moral* criterion; remember, Jesus did not simply *feel* angry when He cleansed the temple, he took action too, wielding a whip in response to the money changers.

Luther described proper anger as acted out in *"meekness, which sorrows over the enemy even while acting in just, temperate action."* Parents may spank in discipline, policemen may use violence to maintain order and enforce the law, soldiers may shoot to kill in battle, and spirited self-defense is permissible. All this is so easy to say when we are sitting around reading a book or having a discussion on a Sunday morning. Unfortunately, in practice, even our purest effort at righteous anger can be tainted with sin. The boundaries some moral theologians set for anger sound as if they have resulted from a consultation with Aristotle:

> Anybody can become angry—that is easy; but to be angry with the right person, and to the right degree, and at the right time, and for the right purpose, and in the right way—that is not within everybody's power and is not easy.[4]

Do you think Aristotle's dictum squares with the teachings of Scripture? Consider Jesus' words: "But I say to you that every one who is angry with his brother shall be liable to judgment; whoever insults his brother shall be liable to the council, and whoever says, 'You fool!' shall be liable to the hell of fire" (Matthew 5:22).

Students of the Bible have found this message very hard to take—so hard that a later copyist made Jesus' words a lot easier to accept by inserting "without a cause" after the word "brother." Though this bit of textual manipulation was done long before the birth of scientific psychology, naturalism, and secularism, I wonder if our preaching, teaching, and counseling on anger might not sometimes involve similar tinkering. Aristotle was right in declaring that righteous anger is not easy; perhaps we psychologists have tried to make it seem as if it is.

What Makes Sinful Anger Sinful?

What then sets *sinful* anger apart from *innocent* anger? Sinful anger is defined as an *inordinate desire for revenge*. When angry revenge is sought *to settle a private score*, the anger is a child of self-centered pride (as are all sins). What if, in addition to feeling the emotion of anger, you also decide to watch for a chance to get even? What if you can't wait to injure someone—emotionally, physically, spiritually, financially, relationally, vocationally—who has hurt you? What if you plan to destroy property? Even to take a life? Or what if you find another person's advantages so far above yours that you enviously determine the situation isn't fair and get so steamed up you insult that person, directly or obliquely, when you find opportunity? What if you never actually do someone else harm in your anger, but instead you daydream about how good it would feel to crunch that person's nose under your fist or say something that would really hurt? Even if you don't actually do any of these things, notice that your anger has become more than a mere emotion gearing you up for self-defense. When you are imagining and looking to get even with someone whom you believe has hurt you, you are sinning.

Inordinate Anger

What is an *inordinate* desire for revenge? This burning wish to hurt another person who has hurt you, a desire so overpowering it can be satisfied only by inflicting injury, is called *malice* in Ephesians 4:31. First, inordinate revenge is sought *without due cause*, violating the principal virtue of justice. (Think of the man who made headlines because he punched an elderly woman for changing lanes in front of him to get to a freeway entrance ramp.) Second, inordinate revenge is revenge sought that is *more severe* than the cause requires. (Think of the multimillion-dollar awards in some product liability suits where there may be a true culpability for injury, but the awards sought are grossly disproportionate to the damage done.) Third, inordinate revenge is revenge that has *hardened into enduring feelings* of resentment, hatred, and spite. (This is called *bitterness* in Ephesians 4:31.)

Some anger is maintained and nurtured; the person nursing it resolves never to let it go. Think of Madame Defarge in Dickens's *A Tale of Two Cities*—a woman who lived each day to foster the French Revolution with the sole personal aim of getting even. Hers was a craving for unlimited bloody vengeance. It was *inordinate* revenge: For the crimes committed against her sister by one single marquis, Madame Defarge sought the guillotine for the entire French aristocracy and all others who showed the slightest sympathy for them. She dedicated her life to the wanton destruction of thousands, so consumed by her anger that anger became her character. Nothing but anger showed in her face—twisted by smoldering resentment and wrath into a perpetual mask of hatred. When anger becomes (and is becoming) an excessive, inappropriate, character-hardening lust for revenge, it is sinful anger.

Deciding to Treasure Angry Character

Earlier I mentioned Nathan; let me now tell you about his case. He was a twenty-seven-year-old graduate student, dark-haired, lean and tall, but too well-muscled to be a geek. He took his seat in my consulting room as if he owned the place and waited for me to ask him why he had come. "What can I do for you today?" I inquired, a little on guard because I had felt his wish to control me reaching across the space between us.

"What can you do for me? Ha! Write my Ph.D. dissertation." (He laughed, expecting me to enjoy the joke. I didn't.) "No, not really; just kidding. I'm having a problem finding a decent relationship. Someone who can fulfill my needs. I have a lot to offer, but I think the available women have been pretty well picked over by the time they reach grad school. They're either man-hating post-feminists or just plain dogs. If a girl comes along who looks pretty good, I get her in bed a few times, and she starts acting like she owns me."

Nathan came off as arrogant, grandiose, and certain that he was entitled to the favors and assistance of others by the mere fact that he existed. He hadn't even uttered ten sentences, and already I did not like him. He had depreciated women—all women. His self-esteem problem was incredible overvaluation of self. Arrogance, one species of the deadly sin of pride, was obviously ingrained in his character. What's more, women for him were a market commodity, and he expected to be allowed to return the merchandise for a full refund at his whim. Talkative to the point of garrulousness, he made it clear that I would not be offered many openings, so I decided to explore a little as soon as I got the chance.

"Tell me about your dissertation—how is that going?"

I must have hit a nerve. "It's a nightmare," he replied. "My advisor is a religion professor who is out to get men. She routinely lets women have complete freedom, but she wants to dictate to me. Wants to force me to accept her interpretation of the data I've come up with, and I don't want to. I should have seen this coming. I have always noticed how religious people ram things down other people's throats. And they usually lack a sense of humor. You've probably noticed it yourself, haven't you? . . . Oh, sorry, I know you're a Christian. . . .

"Well, anyway, I had this tremendous idea for a Ph.D. dissertation. I did an experiment to demonstrate empirically how people become humor-impaired when they get religion. I created a humor test, devised all the items myself, and administered it to two groups—one group was religious and the other was not. I found the groups by using Allport's Intrinsic-Extrinsic Religion scale, which separates people who truly believe from the marginal types. Sure enough, the religious fanatics scored lowest on my humor scales.

"Well, my advisor is very straitlaced. She said my results were not valid because my humor test included too many off-color items. She thought the religious people generated low scores because they were offended. But I say, so what? Wouldn't that still prove they can't take a joke?"

"Hmm. I see. So what are you going to do?"

"I'm going to fight her, that's what! I'm appealing to the committee. I'm sure they'll overrule her. She is the kind that needs to be stopped. If they let her have free rein to trample on student rights, she'll positively drive men out of the religion department! But listen, I came to talk about women. That's where I'm in need of help. I want a relationship. I need some support through these issues, and—well, I need regular sex too. I want you to help me find out why I can't seem to have an enduring relationship. And what can I do about it."

"Would you mind telling me a little about your family?"

"Father, mother, no brothers or sisters. Dad hardly matters. He never said anything, worked hard, spent most of his time away from home. So my mother raised me—if you can call what she did 'raising' me. Mostly she forced me to go to church. She went every time they had a meeting, and I always had to go with her. She was always nagging me to stop this or start that. 'Nathan, have you said your prayers?' 'Nathan, you're cross, and God does not like cross little boys.' She was on a power trip, forcing me to act holy and pious. Until I was eighteen, she insisted on curfews, inspected my room for drugs and other contraband, even read my mail—I suppose she was afraid I might correspond with a girl."

That was all Nathan had to say to reveal his unmitigated spite toward his mother, whose efforts to bend him to her will elicited a sort of sullen hatred rather than rambunctious teenage rebellion. Mother used her "model boy" to show off whenever she could put him on exhibit for her friends. Although it is surely risky to divine her motives through the narrative given by her furious son, it appears that her insistence on Nathan's church attendance and prayers was a way of drawing the praise and approval of others for herself. No, she didn't put him down, didn't crush his self-esteem, didn't cause him to feel unimportant, unwanted, untalented, or any of the more common negative traits children develop in unbalanced homes. Instead,

Nathan grew up angry with his own mother, and because of a phenomenon behaviorists call "generalization," the young man's fury spread to all women. Although I had yet to convince him, his underlying difficulties in relationships were the horrid offspring of his own vengeful wrath.

How to Quit Staying Mad

I want to pause here to discuss an extremely important issue raised by the fact that vindictive anger is a deadly sin. The issue becomes troublesome when we begin to understand the dynamics of Nathan's personality. As I heard about the ruthless determination of Nathan's mother to make her child an adornment for her own ego, I realized of course that I was hearing only his perspective, so I resolved not to judge or condemn her or to say anything negative about her to Nathan. But I also experienced an internal emotional shift familiar to all therapists. My feelings of revulsion toward him became sympathy and understanding.

I began to silently pray, *Father, forgive him, for he does not know what he is doing—yet.* I asked myself, *To what extent is Nathan responsible for his resentment? Can he choose to behave differently, or is he compelled by his "wiring" and his perception that his mother used him for self-aggrandizement to go through life entitling himself to take revenge on others? Does he have a will that he can use to seek the truth about women, to change his self-talk and become a godly man driven no longer by chronic anger?* The answer I received from the Lord was, *Yes, he can do it.*

I remembered others who had done exactly this; wasn't God giving people new birth and new minds every day? Even unbelievers have shown themselves capable of making *behavioral* and *attitudinal* changes in themselves—people like the great Stoic philosopher Marcus Aurelius, the Roman emperor who wrote about cognitive change long before modern psychology discovered the internal monologue. People like Albert Ellis, who has written about and exemplified the ability to deal with feelings of revenge and anger by using his will to change his self-talk. People like some of my own clients who had succeeded in making impressive changes even while they rejected faith.

However, I also know that those who have had to make this journey by using their will without knowing Christ Jesus, and without having the freedom of the will brought by the Holy Spirit dwelling within them through faith in Christ Jesus, have succeeded only *partially* and *never without developing greater pride and sinful confidence in their own excellence.*

Nobody *must* hatefully seek revenge, just as nobody is compelled to sin. Everyone does at times, but nobody *must.* It is this amazing faculty of will that distinguishes human beings from animals, even as the truly *free* will distinguishes the born-anew in Christ from those who do not yet know Him.

Sadly, I did not succeed with Nathan. At first he seemed willing to carefully consider how he might change in order to improve in relationships. But then it became obvious that he would have to forgive his mother and deal effectively with his own self-talk in connection with her admittedly difficult treatment. Moreover, it was crucial for him to mend his frayed relationship with his advisor. Seeing this, Nathan stuck fast to his demand. He wanted my assistance in changing *others.* When *his* need for personal change became the issue, I may have allowed this change to seem too difficult for him. He began to include me among those whom he thought were too religious as well as too envious of his brilliance and attractive personality. One day, after my urging him to change something, he angrily terminated therapy, confirming in his mind his initial assumptions about religious people and their anti-Nathan biases.

Could he have done otherwise? Yes, with the help of God, which is why I grieved over his decisive rejection. Maybe he will one day decide to look at the truth. I have told you about Nathan's anger as an example of how this deadly sin can blind the sinner and prevent insight into its workings. This makes healing difficult but not impossible.

Righteous Anger

I do not believe all anger is wrong, even for us sinful mortals. Righteous indignation is anger aroused by something unjust, mean, or unworthy. Jesus' lashing out at the Pharisees, calling them "whitewashed tombs" (Matthew 23:27), was absolutely just and righteous. True enough, though, as I have said, pure righteous anger for us is rare, the exception to the rule. More often, we mix in elements of personal vendetta, hatred, loveless-ness, and our own pride-warped self's perceived need to destroy someone.

Righteous persons must be especially careful, for it is those who are accustomed to behaving aright who can be caught off guard by a hailstorm of angry emotion. Was it John Calvin's "righteous indignation" that caused him to burn Michael Ser-vetus at the stake in the name of truth? Was Martin Luther "righteously angry" when he called on the Christian nobility to "burn, stab, and slay" the rebellious peasants? They both ar-gued that their actions *were* righteous. Some, even among their ardent followers, have not been so convinced.

Anger by Mouth

Insults are referred to as *evil speaking* or *slander* in Ephesians 4:31. Insults, especially if they are deft sarcasms, witty put-downs, subtle remarks, or cleverly indirect hints, are the partic-ularly ugly progeny of anger. Some people are tremendously skilled at putting others down with veiled cuts, but these jabs are delivered so humorously that bystanders chuckle even though the barb sticks painfully in someone's heart. Sarcastic people may enjoy their own sarcasm, but in reality they are more un-fortunate than their victims. By sinning so insidiously they get an appreciative laugh—they are *rewarded* when they inflict pain, which reinforces the habit of cruelty. In the process they get worse in their sin and move farther along the path to judgment, continuing to repeat their habitual wickedness and hardening themselves until taking another path becomes difficult.

There is also the practice of calling other people insulting names. Not long ago, Dr. Laura Schlessinger, the Jewish radio personality, took on the American Psychological Association for publishing a journal article claiming that pedophilia in some cases is not a disorder and is not harmful to children. For this, she has been bad-mouthed and called *Hitler, Stalin,* and other evil names. Such verbal assaults on truth speakers have become commonplace, and today's media make a practice of publicizing them.

Some people deal out insults that are less direct. I once was presented to an assembly by an angry fellow who admitted that he hated psychology and thought "psychologists are all screwed up." He removed my hard-earned Ph.D. degree by introducing me as "Bill Backus"—even though we had never met and were not on familiar terms. His performance was, I thought, a jaded preamble for my lecture. Such people carry old scores around forever, and for all I know this guy was mad at another therapist he had consulted some years earlier. Anyway, he didn't know me and had no idea what was in my books or what I might have to say. After my talk he asked me if his introduction had irritated me. I replied, "No. Is that what you were trying to do?" Turning beet red, he slipped away without another word.

Quarreling is called *clamor* in Ephesians 4:31. Human beings quarrel about everything, but perhaps the gravest travesty is quarreling about God. Some people seem interested in the Bible only so they can use it to fight about religion. Getting into arguments about church affairs or about doctrine can signal severe disorder, sometimes bordering on paranoia. I was once present at a church meeting in which the quarreling participants gradually worked themselves up to a pitch of anger. Some yelled at the top of their lungs in German, shaking their fists in the pastor's face. All the while they hurled threats and imprecations, quickly turning the sacred assembly into an ugly verbal brawl. I have seen doctrinal discussions of issues such as predestination versus free will become shouting matches. Imagine—shouting matches for the glory of God!

For some individuals, quarreling can be like a contest, a sport, a game played with the equipment of words. Some are experts who get their rewards out of winning—for example, spewing out such anger that others will not dare to pursue their own good points. Some quarreling is conducted with cursing, which is invoking evil upon someone, with a request for God's help. The oft-heard curse is literally a request that God will send someone to hell.

Marital quarrels are so common they occur even in good marriages. In sound relationships, based on mutual love and respect, quarrels happen rarely and are quickly resolved by mutual repentance and resolution to find agreement. But in disordered marriages the quarrels are generally repeated like a script. They are fruitless verbal expressions of anger over chronic issues in which both parties firmly believe themselves right and the other wrong.

Yet these are rarely issues of pure fact, correct reason, or moral truth. More often they are irrational, entangled with hurt and unmet need. Each partner is convinced that he or she has been unfairly and outrageously treated and that the other person's character is dreadful. Such issues can be resolved with real spiritual change in two people who *want* to put away their anger and restore peace and love *more* than they want to win or be right or see the other one get his or her comeuppance. Extremely difficult knots can be untied when *both* parties become spiritually renewed. Marvelous growth can come about through repentance, love, agreements meticulously carried out, and honest assertiveness substituted for indirect aggressive speech.

We will have trouble understanding the Scriptures unless we maintain distinctions between the various kinds of anger. We must acknowledge that there is the pure emotion of anger on the one hand—righteous and Christlike anger, which occurs much less frequently than most of us imagine—and sinful anger that desires or inflicts injury on the other.

Anger for Energy

We have already alluded to one more kind of anger to be considered: anger aroused to energize you, to enable you to help an innocent person who is being injured by an aggressor. Your anger may even include physical aggression if the cause is loving and just and if the physical harm inflicted is proportional to the situation. A fine example of "right rage" is given by the fictional character Nicholas Nickleby, who, in Dickens's great novel by the same name, physically attacks the monstrously cruel schoolmaster Squeers. The scenario: Squeers is brutally beating a poor, vulnerable retarded child nearly to death for committing no offense. And Nickleby, energized by righteous anger, puts Squeers out of action with crippling blows, thereby saving the poor child's life. Righteous anger energizes the loving defense of the endangered innocent even when it involves physical intervention. Those who condemn such anger are incapable of making appropriate distinctions.

Although anger is not abnormal, high scores on the Anger Scale of the Sin Test were positively related to paranoia and schizophrenia. This result does not suggest that anger *causes* paranoia or schizophrenia. Rather it reveals that people with these diagnoses also must frequently cope with sinful anger. Obsessive-compulsive patients also scored significantly on the Anger Scale. Doctors have long noted that there is, in this group of patients, often a streak of hostility. They may sometimes be described as dissatisfied, quarrelsome, irritable, critical, resentful, touchy, rebellious, pugnacious, and/or suspicious. They tend to hold grudges and have difficulty forgiving a slight. Therapists should encourage such patients to work on this aspect of their illness.

The Cure

For our unrighteous anger we need a cure. And we are most likely correct if we seek to rid ourselves of nearly all angry habits. If you have an anger problem, take it seriously; it isn't cute or funny. Anger in most instances is a deadly sin that can become a vicious and damning habit. First, admit your problem—to yourself, to someone else. Stop the habit of denial—"Oh, no, I wasn't *angry*, just a little uncomfortable, just having a bad day, just not thinking . . ."—and admit you have an anger problem, straight out. Second, look away from yourself to the cross where Jesus suffered the whole load of God's wrath to gain forgiveness and a new start in the Holy Spirit for you. Believe this with all your might. Third, promise and plan how you will act to form new habits of love and generosity, understanding and forgiveness. Cultivate the virtue of *meekness*, which is true love for your enemy and for the doer of any evil. Pay attention to the Model: Jesus in His suffering. Imitate Him. For when He suffered, He threatened not (1 Peter 2:23).

Here is advice from Martin Luther's *Treatise on Good Works* (1520):

> Now, since no one lives on earth upon whom God does not bestow an enemy and opponent as a proof of his own anger and wickedness, that is, one who afflicts him in goods, honor, body or friends, and thereby tries whether anger is still present, whether he can be well-disposed toward his enemy, speak well of him, do good to him, and not intend any evil against him; . . . let him set his enemy before him, keep him constantly before the eyes of his heart as an exercise whereby he may curb his spirit and train his heart to think kindly of his enemy, wish him well, care for him and pray for him; and then, when opportunity offers, speak well of him and do good to him. . . .
>
> Where there is true meekness, there the heart is pained at every evil which happens to one's enemy. And these are the true children and heirs of God and brethren of Christ, Whose heart was so pained for us all when He died on the holy Cross. Even so we see a pious judge passing sentence upon the criminal with sorrow, and regretting the death which the law imposes.

Anger in the Sin Test

If you like, you can now test yourself on some of the Anger Scale items from the Sin Test. These items proved statistically to be among the most powerful for measuring the trait indicated by the Anger Scale. Answer True or False.

 _T_   1. I have resentments that I have stored up and harbored for months or years.

F   2. When someone deliberately insults or hurts me, I think for hours about things I should have said or done to get even.

f   3. Frequently I feel frustrated because I cannot think of a way to get even with someone who deserves it.

T   4. Sometimes I get so incensed at what other people do that I just can't control myself.

T   5. I secretly feel good when I learn that someone I dislike has gotten into trouble.

T   6. Too many people in this world get away with wrong-doing.

____ 7. When I think how many stupid people are allowed to drive on our highways, I get angry.

F   8. I really enjoy watching a vicious and bloody boxing match.

T   9. When I read or hear about some of the terrible things other people are getting away with, I am often left with a feeling of outrage and indignation.

T   10. It would make me happy to be able to think up very clever insults toward others when I need to put them in their place.

Examine Your Understanding of Anger

1. Our anger is often legitimate and without sin. True or false, according to John Cassian's teaching?

2. What did Cassian teach would be "a sure remedy for this disease" of anger?

3. In the great play of Euripides, Medea's anger involved taking revenge against her husband, Jason. How did she do this?

4. Luther thought that being angry with others is frequently a good idea. True or false?

5. "Because I feel so upset, I must have been unfairly injured. Therefore my angry reaction is righteous." This is a common way for most of us to justify our anger. Why is this not a reliable indicator that we have every right to be mad?

6. Can you think of an occasion when Jesus, our Example, was angry and showed it? What do you learn from the situation He was in?

7. Anger is a normal response, a provision of the Creator for our good. What is a situation where this response would serve the proper purpose of our Designer?

8. What is "the fight or flight response"?

9. Why is it not all right to take revenge on someone for doing something bad to you?

10. Describe a remedy for a person who has difficulty avoiding the sin of inordinate anger.

For Further Thought and Discussion

---

1. Contrast the anger of Medea with that of Madame Defarge. How were they different from one another? Contrast both of them with the anger of Christ in the New Testament. How were both of these persons different from Christ?

2. The *emotion* of anger is not always sinful because it is a natural biological response to certain situations. Might there be reasons to work at reducing the intensity and the frequency of angry emotions? What would some of them be?

3. Martin Luther wrote concerning a constructive use for enemies: "Since no one lives on earth upon whom God does not bestow an enemy and opponent as a proof of his own anger and wickedness," we ought to . . .

4. On the Sin Test, the Anger Scale did correlate with all the other sins to some extent. However, the highest correlation was with the Pride Scale, and the second highest was with envy. The lowest was with sloth. What might these correlations tell you about anger?

5. Everybody experiences anger, but only certain people are described as angry characters. What makes the difference, and why?

Notes

1. Directed by M. Night Shyamalan.
2. John Cassian, *On Institutes of the Coenobia and the Remedies for the Eight Principle Faults*, book VIII, chapter XXII.
3. Cassian, chapter VII.
4. Aristotle, *Nichomachean Ethics*, chapter 11. Internet citation.

Chapter 5

Greed—Falling in Love
With Possessions

Dan Freeman wasn't a bad guy, nor was Lois, his wife, an evil, troublemaking spouse. From an outsider's perspective, the problem was barely visible. But once the surface was broken, it was clear: Their relationship was suffering from an insidious "greed attack." We'll take a closer look at the Freeman marriage after we learn enough about greed to recognize it in ourselves.

Gehazi wasn't a bad guy either—at least not by today's standards—but he was in a pinch, and the trouble was of his own devising. He was a servant to the prophet Elisha: He helped rescue some down-and-out widows, carried supplies for his master, tended to the cooking and housekeeping, and made himself generally useful to the ministry. Yet a certain character flaw, when it got loose, led to serious consequences. *There is no sense,* Gehazi thought, *in refusing a generous gift when it's offered, the way Elisha did. He must have had his head in the clouds when he sent Naaman* (the healed Syrian leper) *home with his opulent gifts still in his own saddlebags. Indeed, Naaman's love-offering could have been God's way of supplying my needs and those of my master! Why, it's an insult to God to reject the money the Syrian would be delighted to give.*

But just when Gehazi had managed to retrieve the good things, a difficulty emerged. Elisha asked him where he had gone, forcing him to lie. Not dreaming that Elisha knew all about his race to catch up with Naaman (God had allowed Elisha, in the spirit, to see Gehazi in the act of his greedy adventure), Gehazi cooked up a story. He tried to hide the fact that he had conned Naaman by saying that Elisha needed the gift of money and clothes after all, and he had then taken the goods to his own house, thinking nobody would ever know.

Greed led to Gehazi's lying to himself about how this was a "special situation"—about why it was really all right, in this special situation, to take what was not his. Yet it wasn't all right. Greed was a deadly sin then as it is now, having consequences then as it does now, and it earned for Gehazi a lifetime made miserable by leprosy.

Teaching Against Greed

John Cassian asserts that greed "is a regular nest of sins, and a 'root of all kinds of evil,' and becomes a hopeless incitement to wickedness."[1] Greed (or *covetousness*, or *avarice*) also prompts many lines of cautionary teaching in the New Testament: for instance, the horror story of sudden death striking Ananias and Sapphira for hanging on to money while they pretended to have contributed all of it to the common treasury. Such events are recorded not to entertain us but to sound a warning. *When it comes to greed, we all need a danger signal.*

Consider the popularity of a TV show actually named *Greed*, designed to tease out the contestants' covetous impulses. Like no society in history, ours is awash in material abundance. But despite this economic miracle, this generous shower of materialistic bounty, this unprecedented orgy of owning things, most people are far from possessing genuine happiness. Many of us have tried the formula for failure: *The more things you get, the happier you will be.*

Some of us, though, are not yet convinced that happiness and getting things aren't identical. We hear fulfillment equated with acquisition all our waking hours, brainwashing about how contentment flows from procuring *stuff*. We come to believe the nonsense that our spirits will soar through buying this or acquiring that or investing for some promised return. It's not easy to identify with the first readers of Hebrews when we discover that they were joyful because their possessions were ripped off: "You joyfully accepted the confiscation of your property, because you knew that you yourselves had better and lasting possessions" (10:34 NIV).

Let's take a minute to examine the two New Testament Greek words for *greed*, as well as the English synonyms for this lethal sin. Even if looking more closely at single words doesn't usually interest you, try to concentrate your attention on the various nuances in the next couple of paragraphs. It will require some effort right now, but it will help you to recognize and deal with greed in effective ways.

First Timothy 6:10 illuminates a biblical red light, warning us to stop and examine our own avarice. This verse is sometimes twisted to make it say that money is the root of all evil. However, Paul wrote that it is not money but the *love* of money that is synonymous with greed: "For the love of money is the root of all evils; it is through this craving that some have wandered away from the faith and pierced their hearts with many pangs." The Greek word for "craving" is *oregomai*, which draws a verbal sketch meaning, literally, "to stretch forth one's hand." Greed "is a reaching and a grasping. . . . The covetous person . . . lays his hands on anything he can get. He may even snatch away the goods of another. And after he gets them, he clutches them. He is often called tightfisted. Our metaphors for greed/avarice rely inevitably on the arms and hands."[2]

The other New Testament Greek word for greed is *pleonexia*, translated "greed," "avarice," "coveting," or "covetousness." In most contexts, pleonexia means a strong desire to acquire more and more material possessions or to possess more things than other people have, irrespective of need. Do you and your friends admire and envy those who "are experts in greed" (see 2 Peter 2:14 NIV)? Take the wrappings off of greedy desire, and you will find idolatry at its core, since whatever a person fears, loves, and trusts is one's god. "Greed . . . is idolatry" (Colossians 3:5 NIV), and in the case of the greedy person, the god being served is mammon.[3]

From Jesus' own mouth once again, we learn that the sin of greed does not originate with the things we possess but from inside ourselves: "For from within, out of the heart of man, come evil thoughts, fornication, theft, murder, adultery, coveting. . . . All these evil things come from within" (Mark 7:21–23). We need to listen along with Jesus' original hearers, to whom He gave this warning: "Take heed, and beware of all covetousness; for a man's life does not consist in the abundance of his possessions" (Luke 12:15). When we tell ourselves we are greedy because we live in a rich country or because we happen to be prosperous; when we assume that everyone who enjoys material abundance *must* be greedy, we are ignoring the scriptural teaching that *the source of this deadly sin is the heart of a person, not the plentitude of good material gifts one has received.*

Aesop tells of a miser who sold all that he had to buy a lump of gold, which he buried near an old wall and checked daily. One of his workmen observed his frequent visits to the spot and soon discovered the secret of the hidden treasure. Digging down, he came to the lump of gold and stole it. The miser, on his next visit, found the hole empty and began to tear out his hair and to make loud lamentations. A neighbor, seeing him overcome with grief and learning the cause, said, "Pray do not grieve so; but go and take a stone, and place it in the hole, and fancy that the gold is still lying there. It will do you quite the same service; for when the gold was there, you had it not, as you did not make the slightest use of it."[4]

Most tales of truly avaricious characters depict them as burying their money, not spending it. Christian novelist George MacDonald frequently pointed out that it's no sin to have a good deal of wealth. The sin comes from keeping it for no good use, worshiping it as if it were the god mammon, hoarding it and getting one's kicks out of *having* rather than using. Maybe God wants you rich—that's up to Him. But if He does, the point is to find ways to spend for good, for service, and for the meeting of human need.

Personal Greed and the Virtue of Temperance

So how do I recognize greed in myself? The moral theologians agree that greed is the inordinate or excessive desire to acquire in order to possess things, especially wanting more than one needs. Their definitions of these traits, emphasizing *excess* or *overdoing it*, are based on the biblical teachings we just reviewed as well as the *Golden Mean* model of Aristotle's ethics. Aristotle's idea was that many perfectly natural and normal human traits ought not to be missing altogether in a personality, but neither should they be present to an excessive degree. Instead, we ought to aim at the middle way between two extremes: the Golden Mean. The tendency of humans to possess property, for example, is normal and is not evil or wrong. To have too little of the instinct to possess can have ugly consequences— shiftlessness and poverty, for example.

To arrive at the right thing to do, it often works well to avoid both extremes and choose the median. To cheapen and underrate *any* good gift of God, material or otherwise, is sinful. On the other hand, valuing a thing too much—more, say, than you value God or your spouse or one of your children or your neighbor—is sinful greed. We need the *cardinal virtue* of *temperance* (moderation, proportionality) to help us find the middle way, the way of right reason.

Great Tales of Greed

Again, the most extreme form of this vice appears in the classic figure of the miser. In Moliere's *L'Avare*, the avaricious penny pincher, who is greed-incarnate, is given the name Harpagon, which comes from the Greek *harpe*, meaning "claw." Harpagon is a grasping talon, a vicious extension of the human arm and hand. Moliere introduces him immediately, bringing him onto the stage in a state of covetous anxiety and anger at the presence in his house of his son's servant, La Fleche. Harpagon suspects that La Fleche has entered the home to learn where Harpagon has squirreled away his money. Such *total* dedication to getting and hanging on to money or things is rare and extreme enough to be severely deviant. But deviant though this sin may be, it's remarkable how many writers have dealt head on with the issue of extreme greed.

Charles Dickens, for example, who was not poor, left us *A Christmas Carol*, a tale about old Scrooge, a miserable tightwad, finding freedom from the greed that had damned his partner, Jacob Marley. Dickens also gave us the before-mentioned *Nicholas Nickleby*, a magnificent novel in which he introduces us to greedy Ralph, the uncle of Nicholas, who cares for no human soul, only for profits.

Although George MacDonald often addressed greed, he rarely used misers to portray it. More often, his illustrations involved well-off members of the nobility. In *The Marquis' Secret*, for example, Clementina, a snobbish, well-to-do English heiress, loses her heart and her love for mammon through a life-changing meeting with Jesus Christ.

Greed also furnishes the theme for John Grisham's blockbuster novel *The Testament*. The story opens with the suicide of a cantankerous old multibillionaire whose surprising, handwritten will torpedoes the sanguine expectations of his three dissipated ex-wives, their malign offspring, and their avaricious attorneys. Shockingly, he deeds his entire eleven-billion-dollar fortune not to this flock of buzzards but to a poor missionary in the remote wilds of Brazil. The corrupt relatives aren't misers but rapacious birds of prey, competing with each other for the inheritance. Their craving for money drives them to tear themselves and one another to shreds. The story shows us a carnival of covetousness, hatred, and selfishness with few equals in contemporary fiction, leaving the reader thoroughly disgusted with the loathsome greed of this rich man's family.

Yet alongside this disgust we ought to do some self-searching: "Would I, if I were in their shoes, drool over having and holding on to eleven billion dollars? Would my motivations and actions change? Would I drop or lower my standards? Would I try to push God aside and go my own way? Would I believe I needed Him at all?" Grisham skillfully brings us to heel by the appearance of a character so Christlike that she has absolutely no interest in money and refuses point-blank to accept the no-strings-attached bequest.

To Find Your Greed, Follow Your Heart

"But I'm no miser," I used to tell myself when I ran across such extremes. "I don't have to worry about being greedy." Well, it's not that simple. True, most of us are not cheapskates, nor presumptive heirs to billions. Yet with us greed often appears in less extreme or less obvious forms. Because of its overall prevalence, the deadly sin of greed is hardly noticeable in a society as materially rich as ours. With affluence all around us, could it be that in denying the possibility of greed in ourselves we are comparing ourselves with the culture's standards rather than God's? Could it be that instead of seeking to eliminate our greed altogether, we are content merely to be "lower on the Greed Scale" than those in our midst?

Rather than simply loving money to the exclusion of all else, we may cater to it more than we ought, pursuing money or the feel of it in our hands, currying favor in the hopes of financial dividends, savoring the look and texture of stocks and bonds, gazing at the totals in our savings accounts, collecting or owning just for the sensation of possessing. And remember, it's not just about money! *This* is greed: living to possess *anything*—stamps, dolls, autographed balls, books, CDs, paintings, figurines, toys, property, cars, contacts/acquaintances, whatever—with the primary objective of owning, the preoccupation with having, the obsession of getting, and/or the dedication of too much of our lives or the investment of too much of our hearts. "Where your treasure is, there will your heart be also," said Jesus in Luke 12:34.

Of course, not all desiring is coveting. *Coveting* is wanting things in a certain way—it is a warped wanting, forbidden in the ninth and tenth commandments, and not just any kind of desire. It is *all-consuming*, a fixation on what belongs rightly to someone else, whether it be money, house, land, or anything else. To go beyond the recognition that the person or object is truly attractive, to proceed to the point where you imagine possessing it, plan to obtain it, figure ways to get it, become obsessed with the burning passion to *have* it—this is greed.

As with other sins, our own greed isn't easy to see. We may have a hard time, for instance, discriminating between the virtue of *prudence* and the sin of *avarice*. We want to be generous givers, but how can we know what amount to give? What size gift is truly generous, and what amount is so large as to be foolhardy? We don't know what tomorrow will bring or what unforeseen emergency will cost huge sums and catch us with insufficient resources. In retaining some while giving the rest, how can we perceive the difference between assertive prudence on the one hand and possessive greed on the other?

Sometimes we are accused of greed by those who believe they are more entitled to the fruits of our labors than we are. Such fault-finding, though it grows out of the accuser's own greed, can fill the innocent with self-doubt even when it is utterly false. *What if it's true?* we wonder with apprehension. After all, covetousness, like all the deadly sins, lurks within every one of us in some measure, seeking its own way. We want to love God, but we may find we care too much about upgrading our own standard of living; we actually can end up trying to do both—doing a balancing act to "serve God and mammon" (Matthew 6:24). This problem is worse for those who have great possessions than for the very poor who have hardly enough to afford them a significant amount of choice in the matter of how much to give and how much to keep. But it is a problem for *each* person to take seriously into heart-searching prayer and openness to the voice of the Holy Spirit.

Envy and Greed: The Difference

An interesting antithesis exists between envy and greed. While the envious have sinful attitudes *toward* possessions, the greedy character places ultimate value on *possessions themselves* and feels good while in the act of obtaining the belongings of others. The envious person, in contrast, values a thing and covets it *while* it belongs to someone else. The act of taking possession renders it worthless, for all that is his automatically appears trashy compared to the things of others.

The Motivating Power of Greed

Take a youngster who thinks it is totally beneath him to perform the light chores assigned by his parents. He sees no purpose in the effort, and thus he refuses to put it forth. As he grows up, however, he earns money for his efforts, so his perspective turns completely around. Discovering that work pays off, he dedicates himself to gain. John Cassian comments on how terrifyingly motivating greed could be, even in the life of an ancient monk: "This dedication to possessions forces him to labor without stopping night and day . . . suffers him to keep no services of prayer, no . . . seemly intercession, if only he can satisfy the madness of avarice . . . inflaming the more the fire of covetousness, while believing that it will be extinguished by getting."[5]

The Grip Strengthens

The observation that avarice gets worse with age seems to have been recorded first by St. Thomas Aquinas. Older people *have* scored higher than younger people on the Greed Scale of the Sin Test. Today it could be that the fear of want, the sad news that the cost of living always outstrips Social Security payments, and the onset of greater bodily weakness and physical incapacitation motivate some to hang on even more tightly to earthly resources. Such concerns naturally tend to increase as life passes.

But these factors aren't always the motivators, for greed usually doesn't "disappear" when needs get met—*more* is still desired. "Successful" greed can create what Cassian called "a veritable nest of sins," because the love of money is the root out of which many other sins can sprout. If a reasonably able person with good self-control sets his mind on getting and saving (and even hoarding) wealth, then the probability of becoming rich may be quite high. Again, "those who desire to be rich fall into temptation, into a snare, into many senseless and hurtful desires that plunge men into ruin and destruction" (1 Timothy 6:9). Having more money than you need can lead to arrogance, showing off, free rein to lust, unbridled pursuit of entertainment, frequent or constant desire for illicit pleasure, and proud condescension toward people who have less—among other things.

Wealth is not the cause of greed. One who actually has no money may still be greedy, even more greedy than a person of moderate means! As a matter of fact, patients in the psychiatry ward of a county hospital tended to have higher Greed Scale scores on the Sin Test than the other groups tested. This result might be related to the fact that many of the patients in this particular unit occupied marginal economic status. How could this elicit greed? It is plausible that involuntary poverty may cause a person to think a great deal about money and possessions, just as fasting might cause a person to think a great deal about food. This means that *covetousness is not the same as possessing things*; it is a craving, a grasping, a disposition of the heart, an attitude toward possessions whether or not you have them.

How to Identify Greed

What are the behaviors and attitudes of greedy people? Sometimes greed shows up as a refusal to engage in any pursuit except materially profitable occupations, a stinginess in the use of material things or in paying debts, a penuriousness in choosing what to buy and when. It can also be saving at the expense of common necessities, feeling miserly distress over trifling losses, close-fistedness in giving, willingness to employ dishonest and unjust means to get and keep possessions—even anger at being compelled to look upon the importunity of poor people.

Does Society Approve or Not?

Is the popularity of avarice dying out? The Great Depression brought about a surge in promotion of thrift and frugality, and with this came social approval of some forms of greed. "Waste not, want not," said our boarding school chef, Cookie. She was careful not to throw away anything that might be even the slightest bit useful, night after night serving us warmed-over spaghetti without much, if any, sauce. In those days, savings accounts were sponsored at school for children who would bring their pennies and nickels to their teacher, who would then deposit them on the youngsters' behalf. With so much emphasis on thrift, we were taught Ben Franklin's maxims and learned to view thrift as a near-biblical virtue. Small wonder that greed was so easily overlooked.

Until about 1968, the cultural climate in America, for the most part, maintained its tacit approval of greed. People who pursued unlimited wealth for its own sake were often admired as exemplary. Amassing money, succeeding with investments, and doing well in business were subjects one could talk about in social situations without suffering disapprobation—indeed, others sought to emulate and admire the wealthy and powerful.

But then something changed, beginning with the young. Remember the curious phenomenon of the cultural revolt? Many of the youth—children of the affluent—advertised their scorn for the pursuit of wealth. Some proudly disdained employment or careers; in *The Graduate*, Dustin Hoffman's character, at home with his well-to-do parents throughout much of the summer after graduation from college, appears virtually culture-shocked. But when the dust settled and the protesters grew to maturity, they turned out at least as greedy as any other generation. The remedy for sin does not come from denouncing the sins of others.

Generosity Heals

Why do we need to be cured of greed? Because greed is bad—not merely a negative factor but *deadly* for us. Scripture describes at least three human catastrophes due to greed, of which we've already referenced two. When Gehazi, Elisha's servant, tried to get the money Elisha had turned down, not only did he fail to obtain the gift of prophecy, which he would have received from his master by hereditary succession, but he was covered from head to foot by incurable leprosy. Judas, craving wealth, bought it with a kiss. Through greed he fell into betraying the Lord, lost his apostolic rank, suffered misery of spirit, and died a violent, self-inflicted death. Ananias and Sapphira, lying to keep back a part of what was their own anyway, were punished with instantaneous death. *Greed harms the greedy.* It causes anxiety by directing our trust to a thing that is here today and gone tomorrow instead of to Him who lives and reigns to all eternity.

But *generosity heals*. One of the major health effects of Christian charity is this: It forces our greedy claws to let go of something. To give, we must loosen our clenched fists. Why do we give? Because we need to—for our spiritual (and mental) health! No way does God need our money or things; He already owns them *and* us. But we have a *need* to relax our grip because maintaining such a rigid hold on things creates major stresses; our own healing requires us to relinquish the vise of the "greed grasp." Generous giving is a marvelous exercise for spiritual and psychological wholeness, *not* a terrible law by which God deprives us of our precious possessions.

Dan and Lois: Victory Over Greed

The Freemans, to whom we have already been introduced, were an attractive, energetic couple with relationship troubles. Lois was a full-time housewife and mother of four. Dan, an industrial psychologist, was a trainer for managers, teaching other people to communicate. When I read on their registration form that they had come to see me for marriage counseling, I thought, *At least these people won't tell me they're having communication problems.* Oops.

"We don't seem to be able to communicate," Dan began with a straight face. This is a routine opener for people in conflict. Normally, it's only a way of getting started, easier than admitting to a lot of quarreling. Dan and Lois would not mention the matter of communication again; instead, they would have to tell me about the distressing behavior that propelled them to a third person for help. One or the other would risk describing the rift. I listened.

"I want to know if it's fair for Dan to keep our money in his own bank account," said Lois, with a smile pasted on to cover the tension in her face.

No reasonably peace-loving therapist would answer such a question even if it had an answer, so I kept quiet and pondered the dynamics of money and greed in marriage while I waited to see what would happen next.

When Lois realized that I would not act as their referee, she continued. "He gives me an allowance that is supposed to cover all our groceries, clothes, and anything else I might need to buy. But I feel like . . . like he thinks I'm a child. Like in his eyes I have no discretion. Is that fair, Doctor? Wouldn't it be more realistic for us to have a joint account so I could write checks when I need to? We don't need to be chintzy. Dan makes a good living. I feel like he's penny-pinching with me."

Dan had been quiet while Lois made her point, but now he'd had enough. His own avaricious flesh demanded a hearing: "I give her plenty of money." Turning to his wife, he delivered his own assessment (which was not by any means news to her): "Lois, anybody ought to be able to manage a household with what I let you have every month."

I realized I was hearing some of their "old refrains," dialogues they had repeated countless times in bedroom and kitchen, material that involved unleashing their sinfulness. I pondered how Dan's anxiety made him insecure and how Lois suffered from difficulties with boundaries, but it would be a mistake to assign all this trouble to personality traits without recognizing the role of plain human greed.

Dan continued: "You know what would happen if you had unfettered access to our checking account. You would forget to record some of your checks and I wouldn't have the slightest idea what our balance is. Imagine the mess we would have and what a big swamp I'd run into every month when I reconcile our accounts. You're a wonderful woman, but you just don't handle money well, Sweetheart. You know, Dear, I give you almost half my income as it is. I don't see why, but no matter how much I give you, you want more. You want *all* of it, don't you?"

Dan's effort at soft-soaping Lois had no effect. She had heard it all before, and she replied indignantly that it wasn't true that she wanted "more" and that Dan wasn't *giving* her any-thing—that household expenses weren't exclusively *hers*. He insisted that what he *gave* her (retaining and even emphasizing the irritating verb) was more than enough not only for expenses but also for impulse spending. She, now nearly shouting, convincingly invited him to run the home if he thought it was so easy.

Dan then resurrected the historical material most bickering spouses eventually run by each other to cinch their argument. Assuming all the authority his profession bestowed on him, he advised Lois, "Your problem stems from your mother. She spent everything your father earned and then some. They almost went bankrupt. Remember?"

Lois had learned long ago that two can play this game, and that, even if she wasn't a psychologist like Dan, her gender, with its superior memory for certain classes of information, was convinced she could win it. She reminded him of his own parents' perpetual arguments over money.

Nothing either one of them said or did was novel or refreshing. They had been over this ground until it was trampled to concrete. Here, in the presence of a third person, they tried, barely, to display more courtesy than they managed when they squabbled at home. I listened to another round or two, knowing that all this was being rerun for my benefit. Lois was soon in tears. Dan's eyes glistened with barely restrained fury. I would have to help them to change directions.

"Do you see what you are doing?"

Dan replied, "Yeah, we're not getting anywhere."

Lois added, "Just like always."

"Like always! And why is that?" I asked, responding to my own question before they could take up the cudgels again. "Because when you discuss money, greed takes over in each of you. There was probably a time when you both saw to it that your loving spirits motivated your interactions, and the result was that each of you subordinated every selfish, sinful impulse to your desire to please and fulfill the other. You really lived out what God says of married people: You two are one! Remember the results? You basked in one another's joy, laughter, peace, and fulfillment. As a result you were in love." (They both nodded their agreement, smiling slightly to think how passionately in love they had once been.)

"Then something happened: Your sinful flesh began to generate greed, and greed leads to fear—fear that you might lose out because you were giving so much to the other; fear that you weren't getting your fair share; fear that if you kept this up you would be played for a loser. Instead of being one flesh you became adversaries over money. It doesn't matter which one of you started this contest, because the greedy flesh of your spouse responded in kind. Pretty soon, you were both caught in a trap of greed, like the snare of sin Paul describes in Romans. To be a healed couple, you must both stop letting greed make you enemies. Instead of battling *each other's* greed, you must smother *your own.* Now let me ask you, do you know for certain that you have new natures, born of the Spirit of God?"

Dan and Lois both insisted they had new natures, that they knew the Lord Jesus lived in their spirits. I helped them to realize that what each one really wanted as renewed spiritual persons was the other's contentment and happiness. We established that they would have to work out a way to love and care for one another with their new nature's generosity. And to do this they would have to formulate a pattern for dealing with their income in a manner where each would be meeting the other's needs.

"I'm sure you can see," I continued, "that doing this will be difficult, will take effort, and will require that you both spend a lot of time at getting along. And I'm sure you can also see what has to happen to greed with its fleshly, 'get mine and do it my way' rule. It must lose out to the way of the Spirit. Instead of clashing, bitterness, and enmity, you will experience once again the bliss of being yoked together and loving and serving one another."

They were willing. I showed them how to apply the three principles spelled out in chapter 1: *(1) The principle of checking internal speech,* and replacing the bad with the good, the distorted with the truth; *(2) The principle of choosing incompatible behavior;* and *(3) The principle of making moral choices with zealous determination.*

Dan and Lois agreed to work on their greed and the role its underlying misbeliefs had been playing in their relationship. They also decided to choose a new program of more generous giving to others because *loving and giving are not compatible with greed.* Once they understood that they would have to make new moral choices in their dealings with each other, they agreed to make these changes with determination and zeal.

In this instance, I have compressed dialogue that took place over several sessions; much had to be repeated and reiterated. The Freemans made good starts, then regressed several times. But they finally succeeded in suppressing their flesh and working with the aim of generous love applied to each other's requests. They progressed constructively toward solutions. Both of them found the solutions not only acceptable but congenial. So as not to leave you wondering, here is what they finally did:

Dan agreed to a joint bank account on which Lois too could write checks. This satisfied her, but left Dan with his fears, objections, and insecurities that the couple had to resolve. What about her habit of forgetting to record her checks? After conferring with their banker, they found there was an easy solution: They ordered new checkbooks that made a carbon copy of every check. Problem solved. But the solution was made possible because by repentance and decisions made in faith, these people removed their greed from its position of control and gave the love and generosity of their spirits free rein. Dan and Lois had other issues that they worked on in similar fashion. Yet what was most delightful to both of them was the success they saw in taming their greedy natures and experiencing their renewed life in the Spirit. Like newlyweds, they found themselves enjoying their love again.

Perhaps most readers will find their own greed more resembles that of Dan and Lois than the avarice of Scrooge or Judas. But the remedy is the same: If we live by the Spirit, we need to walk by the Spirit (Galatians 5:25).

The More Excellent Way

The remedy for greed must be capable of changing us from the inside out. Unless it alters our desires as well as our actions, denouncing greed can only bring about guilt and resentment. *True virtue includes internal as well as external goodness.* Of the three theological virtues (faith, hope, and charity), the greatest is charity (1 Corinthians 13:13 KJV). This belongs first and foremost to God and only derivatively to us. But because of God's generous love, His abundant giving, we can be empowered by faith to become generous ourselves, practicing the gift of charity with our possessions. "Herein is love," says John, "not that we loved God, but that He loved us, and sent His Son to be the propitiation for our sins" (1 John 4:10 KJV). Nothing can ever top what God has done, and by doing it, God acting in Christ empowers us to imitate His generosity.

God in Christ is also our model for developing the virtue of charity. "Love one another. As I have loved you," Jesus tells us (John 13:34 NIV). Those who want to grow in virtue and die to sin must know Jesus—not merely with formal assent to His Godhead and Kingship, but also by immersion in His person, character, and teaching. We can hardly become *like* Him without becoming *acquainted* with Him. No greed at all lurked in His breast. He set the standard for its opposite: He gave even His own life for others.

Check the internal speech misbeliefs that urge you to focus your life on getting more and hanging on to all you can get. What are you telling yourself? That God won't take care of you, so you have to look out for yourself? Replace that and other greed-generating misbeliefs with the truth that a loving Father will not be stingy with His child; you must believe this before you can obey Him in love and generosity. Practicing obedience to Christ's command that we love our neighbor involves *the principle of incompatible behavior.* When we are generously giving in Spirit-inspired charity, it's difficult to practice selfish greed at the same time. And finally, convince yourself to love and give with *zealous determination.*

Greed in the Sin Test

If you like, you can now test yourself on some of the Greed Scale items from the Sin Test. These items proved statistically to be among the most powerful for measuring the trait indicated by the Greed Scale. Answer True or False.

F 1. If the credit department of a store to which I owe money should forget to bill me, I would simply figure that it's their problem.

F 2. I keep myself so busy that I rarely have time to think about God and religion.

F 3. I couldn't care less what people think of me as long as I have plenty of money.

T 4. I would prefer a high-paying job in which I was less interested to a lower-paying job that interested me very much.

F 5. When I lose money I get so uncomfortable I can hardly think about anything else.

F 6. Quite often I do things like buy winter coats or Christmas toys during the summer because of the satisfaction of getting them at half price.

F 7. If I knew I could get away with it, I would do something I knew to be wrong to acquire a substantial sum of money.

_T_ 8. One of my major goals· in life is to accumulate enough money so I can be sure of a secure future.

_F_ 9. I would rather have a life rich in the knowledge and fellowship of God than a basement full of gold.

_T_ 10. I would especially enjoy collecting and owning fine and expensive things (for example, furniture, books, jewelry, art objects).

Examine Your Understanding of Greed

1. Do you think that anybody who wants to try can practice the Christian virtue of *charity*? Why or why not?

2. Why do we need to relax our greedy hold on material things in order to enjoy more complete healing?

3. Do you think that the more things you possess the happier you will be? Is it possible to *think* this idea is false and yet *live* as though it is true?

4. Explain how the love of money can be the root of other evils and why money itself is neither evil nor the root of evils.

For Further Thought and Discussion

1. One of life's hard questions is this: "How can I know when I have enough and when I can and should stop striving for more security when there are so many unknowns?" How do you deal with this issue?

2. Read Isaiah 5:8 (KJV): "Woe unto them that join house to house, that lay field to field, till there be no place, that they may be placed alone in the midst of the earth!" Read also Habakkuk 2:6 (KJV): "Shall not all these take up a parable against him, and a taunting proverb against him, and say, Woe to him that increaseth that which is not his! how long? and to him that ladeth himself with thick clay!" Who today ought to be cautioned by such passages as these? Is there a warning here for ordinary Christians?

3. True or false?—One thing is clear: The great advances in science and technology over the past three hundred years have enabled us to live happy lives—we are clearly much happier than people used to be. Do you agree? What do you think your conclusion demonstrates?

Notes

1. John Cassian, book VII, chapter VI.
2. William F. May, *A Catalogue of Sins: A Contemporary Examination of Christian Conscience* (New York: Holt, Rinehart, and Winston, 1967), 52.
3. *Mammon* is a word meaning "wealth" or "property."
4. *Aesop's Fables*, trans. George Fyler Townsend. http://classics.mit.edu/Aesop/fab.html.
5. Cassian, http://www.osb.org/lectio/cassian/inst/index.html.

Chapter 6

Sloth—Depression or Laziness? Sickness or Sin?

Strange as it seems, what finally drove Ben to consult a psychologist was a chance event: He happened to glance at a certain book in the Bible. A day off work with nothing to do was the last thing he needed—at least so he told himself as he cast about in his mind for some way to fill up the lonely hours. Time—an entire day—stretched out before him as an endless eternity.

But he couldn't think of any activity worth the effort required to do it. "Here I am with a holiday and nothing to do," he groaned, lamenting the aching emptiness he felt in himself. He felt a yearning for a close friend he might talk to or perhaps a woman he might just walk with around the lakes or plan a picnic with or . . . *Well, what was the use?* Ben couldn't think of a single person he wanted to spend the day with. "Why bother?" he grumbled. "I don't have any friends who would understand." He knew there were women who would have been delighted to spend the day with him, but none of the names on his mental Rolodex stirred any interest. All his male acquaintances were working. The kids were at school, and anyway, he couldn't unburden himself to them. His mood, gloomy to begin with, turned bitter, even resentful. God, Whoever He was, *if* He existed, had destroyed him. Truly, there was nothing left. He couldn't imagine being contented with anybody—or for that matter he couldn't think of anything he wanted to do.

Downcast, he began thumbing through the big Bible his wife had given him for one of his birthdays long ago. It was like new, since Ben had rarely opened it. Turning idly through the pages, his eye fell on a book with an odd name: Ecclesiastes. He paged through it briefly.

"Well, whoever decided this should be in the Bible must have been having a rotten day—like I am," he muttered, strangely consoled by the author's opening complaints: "Vanity of vanities, vanity of vanities! All is vanity."

Ben found these denunciations of just about everything oddly comforting. He read on: "What does man gain by all the toil at which he toils under the sun?" (The Preacher, as Solomon, the author, calls himself, had gotten Ben's attention.) "Yep," he found himself agreeing, almost in tears, "this guy sure makes his point. It's like he knows what I'm thinking—like his view of life agrees with mine. At least somebody in the Bible understands what a raw deal some of us get. This guy knows it—how poor, innocent people always get ripped off, how there's no justice anywhere, how evil wins over good as often as not, and how at the grand finale, you end up in a box in the ground.

"He sounds like he asks my question, 'Where is God?' Answer: 'Not anywhere you'd notice.' (I can't believe this stuff is in the *Bible!* By a *preacher!*) He says he tried everything: laughing, learning, accomplishing, affluence, romance, even foolishness. He put a lot of effort into gaining wisdom. All he got out of it was a lot of nothing—no happiness, no satisfaction, no fulfillment, really.

"That's where I am, too. I agree with him: The dead are lucky; they don't have to go through any more of this useless life. My life is worthless to me—probably because I'm worthless. There's no hope." Ben went on reading until he couldn't stand it, closed the book, and broke down in tears. *I need somebody to talk to,* he thought, *or else I'm going to—to . . .*

Ben's mind painted pictures sometimes, like now. He saw himself starting his car in the garage with the door closed, sitting quietly in the driver's seat, inhaling lethal fumes, drifting gently away, away from all the vanity—and pain. It all looked so good. *But what about the kids,* he heard his own voice arguing against the suicidal thoughts, *Patrick and Laura. They would be scalded emotionally, so soon after losing their mother, a second loss for them to manage. Better talk to someone.* He thought he had cried all his tears beside Miriam's casket. But his loss was an aching void and he'd been crying a lot lately. Today something had un-dammed a deluge. By this time, his weeping made it hard to look up the phone number of the psychologist he had heard once at Miriam's church.

He felt a little better just making the appointment. And he was doing *something* about his situation. Even if it didn't help, at least he would be going in a direction more constructive than planning his own self-destruction.

When Ben told me his story and came to the part about Ec-clesiastes, I felt a twinge in my solar plexus! Although he was in deep distress, seriously depressed, God was at work and He had used this book to bring Ben back from the brink of despair.

Ben's depression included the characteristics of the deadly sin of sloth. There was the faint spirit, the heaviness, the lack of desire to accomplish much of anything, the dejection, the sor-row, the oppressive grief, the feeling that effort is useless, and the utter hopelessness of life. Self-devaluation, too. *The clinical diagnosis of depression and the spiritual diagnosis of sloth would both be appropriate.* But the spiritual diagnosis would highlight the moral and spiritual morass out of which Ben would have to be delivered through coming into fellowship with God through Jesus' atoning blood.

Was Ben simply depressed, a victim of a *purely psychological ailment?* Or was there a *spiritual* component, even a *moral* factor involved? The ancient writers on such things would have re-sponded that this condition involves all three of those factors: psychology, spirituality, and morality. And they had a different name for what afflicted Ben: *sloth*. How can it be that depression and sloth go together, may even be the same disorder called by different names? Is it cruel of God to look upon our despair and inner misery and call it a deadly sin? No. For God suffers when we suffer. Our pain is His pain. And the part of us that lies back on our bed of pain and gives up, telling ourselves we're no good, there's no hope, and life is not worth living, God does all He can to change by bringing us to repentance and truth. Read on. You'll see what I mean.

It was St. John Cassian's fourth-century delineation of sloth that first attracted my attention to the Seven Deadly Sins. Before my internship supervisor, Dr. Tom Kiresuk, directed my focus toward Cassian's clinical-sounding description, I had given no attention at all to this ancient list of unwelcome character traits. As for sloth itself, I had always assumed it was plain old laziness. But on closer examination, sloth turned out to be much more complex than a banner for do-nothing deadbeats.

> Our sixth combat is with what the Greeks call *acedia* which we may term weariness or distress of heart. This is akin to dejection, and is especially trying to solitaries, and a dangerous and frequent foe to dwellers in the desert; and especially disturbing to a monk about the sixth hour, like some fever which seizes him at stated times, bringing the burning heat of its attacks on the sick man at usual and regular hours. Lastly, there are some of the elders who declare that this is the "midday demon" spoken of in the ninetieth Psalm.[1]

What Cassian (and the other elders[2] he refers to) saw in the afflicted monk was not mere unwillingness to work but also emotional *torment*, enduring *anguish*. Some of his contemporaries saw sloth as a *demonic attack*, and Cassian himself speaks of the slothful person as *the sick man*. If we take this literally, then we must conclude that what the desert fathers named *sloth* is a psychological state or trait that includes elements of sin, demonic affliction, and illness. The more we learn about what the ancients called sloth, the more it appears that sloth is today labeled clinical depression. Assuming that sloth is a *kind* of depression, we might gain from the fathers a fuller grasp of this serious and widespread disorder.

Scripture on Sloth

Let's begin with the biblical teachings. The Old Testament Greek[3] term for sloth was *acedia*. In classical Greek, acedia means "without care, careless, heedless." But in our English Bibles acedia is translated with such expressions as "a faint spirit" or "the spirit of heaviness" (KJV). For instance, in Isaiah 61:3, acedia is rendered "heaviness," as in "the garment of praise for the spirit of heaviness." In Proverbs the word usually refers to avoidance of one's appropriate work; for example, "A slothful man will not catch his prey" (12:27).

The New Testament Greek term for sloth is *hokneeros*, which means "shrinking from" or "hesitating to engage in something worthwhile," possibly implying "lack of ambition" or "laziness." For example, Matthew 25:26: "But his master answered him, 'You wicked and slothful (*hokneere*) servant!' " Or Romans 12:11: "Never flag in zeal (*hokneeroi*), be aglow with the Spirit, serve the Lord."

The Latin word for sloth used by St. Thomas Aquinas and some others is *tristitia*, meaning "sorrow." For Aquinas the accent in "sloth" was somewhat different. The emphasis was on the painful feelings that sloth includes. (Our English word "sloth" comes from the Middle English term *slou*, or "slow.") If this seems odd to you, try to remember when you were sorrowful and felt you could hardly move for lack of energy. Sorrow and heaviness do, in fact, seem to go together.

Summing up, then, this deadly sin is a spiritual/psychological/medical package that includes elements of listlessness, heaviness, apathy, lack of ambition, lack of zeal, dejection, and sorrowful emotional states. You can see that this sin trait includes far more than mere external laziness. How did we ever come to the point where the idea of sloth was reduced to this alone?

With the burgeoning of industry and the work ethic accompanying the Industrial Revolution, some moral theologians began to equate sloth with simple resistance to work. But there is more, *much* more to sloth than inactivity. As the trait originally called sloth is today called *depression*, I will treat the two words as synonyms from this point forward.

Sloth and Sadness

Contemporary psychologists have, for the most part, lost the understanding of Aquinas, who defined this vice as a genuinely *theological* sin, that is, a sin directly against God. (See chapter 2 for John Cassian's view of directly theological sin.) He called it *tristitia de bono spirituali*, "sadness in the face of spiritual good."[4]

Remember how Ben felt resentment against God even though he wasn't even sure there was such a Being? Later we will look at the case of Amelia and examine her self-talk about God. For her, sloth involved declaring that God was not doing her any good at all—*if* He even existed. Sometimes believers experience sloth as an attitude of alienation from God. Accepting the testimony of their lackadaisical lethargy, they tell themselves that God has left them altogether. But this is never so; the condition of sloth is man's disorder, not God's.

John of Damascus,[5] one of the great teachers of the Eastern Church, defines this sin as "oppressive grief."[6] He noticed a fascinating relationship between envy and sloth in that *both* involve feelings of sorrow (tristitia): Envy is sorrow in the face of another person's good fortune, while sloth is sorrow in the face of one's own good God.[7]

How People Experience Sloth Today

Individuals vary in the particular symptoms they describe to their therapists, relatives, or friends. While a few sit down and say, right off, "I'm depressed!" others say, "I'm having trouble thinking—it's like my mind has slowed down." Some begin with, "I can't sleep." Many, like the church leader I talked to recently, complain that they just don't have any energy, enthusiasm, or "get-up-and-go." A depressed grandmother told me, "I can't cook, I can't do my needlework anymore, I can't go anywhere—I don't feel like doing anything. I'm dragged out and tired all the time." A marketing expert said, "I can barely get myself out of bed in the morning." And an extremely sociable young woman didn't want to see any of her friends, even though being alone made her miserable. They all agree: "Sloth is not a pretty picture."

Inwardly, sloth is felt as grief, dejection, listlessness, restlessness, and psychic exhaustion. You feel that everything around you is distasteful, repulsive. Your life is boring and unendurable, the days are far too long, and your work is unbearable. You are a burden to yourself, and your thoughts contain self-deprecation, which is anything but Christian humility because it does not rest on the truth—*the truth* leads to ministering meekness and lowliness of heart. Other expressions used by theologians to describe acedia: weariness or distress of heart, disquiet, desire to "get away," restlessness, idleness, somnolence,[8] boredom, sadness, and lukewarmness. Internal joy and sweetness have gone and now are replaced by self-directed anger, despair, anxiety, loathing, bitterness, and inner drought.[9]

The great Rhabanus Maurus[10] described the slothful Christian as cheerless in spiritual works, with no joy in the salvation of his soul. This poet-scholastic added the arresting note that sloth makes a person dull in carnal desires (i.e., having little interest in sex); such complaints are commonly heard today from depressed patients.

If we boil down this collection of descriptive terms, we are left with two elements. First, depression involves feelings of sadness, heaviness, and dullness, along with hopelessness and the melancholy conviction that life has no meaning. In our psychologically-oriented society, absorbed as we are with our own subjectivity and the overweening importance of our feelings, we avoid the term sloth and prefer the term depression. To us, the important feature seems to be the *feelings* of sadness (*tristitia cordis*). Second, depression also involves aversion to effort, and the moral danger of sloth lies in this characteristic. The work

involved in exercising one's will to make moral and spiritual decisions seems particularly undesirable and demanding. Thus the
slothful person drifts along in habits of sin, convinced that he
has no willpower and aided in this claim by those who persist in
seeking only biological and environmental causes and medical
remedies for sloth.[11]

Sloth and Sinful Behavior

Some slothful characters may procrastinate habitually, putting off important duties and distracting themselves with insignificant activities, chattering, gossiping, or even sitting and
staring at the wall. To keep from worrying about her failures to
perform, the slothful person occupies herself with valueless in-
volvements, perhaps passively watching whatever happens to
flicker across the TV screen, or lounging for hours in front of
the computer, or sometimes simply remaining inactive, thinking
about her losses, shortcomings, and pains. "I can't make myself
write that term paper!" the student complains. "I can't" is a
phrase to examine carefully if you're using it, especially in view
of Paul's triumphant claim, "I can do *all* things in him who
strengthens me" (Philippians 4:13, emphasis added).

Sometimes we encounter someone who ministers to depressives by informing them, "Know what's the matter with you?
You're just full of self-pity." This is an irresponsible snap judgment, much too narrow a diagnosis, a glaring instance of judg-
ing and condemning, and an oversimplification that to my
knowledge has not been helpful.

As we have seen, sloth is clearly not simple laziness, as laziness is commonly understood. As a recovering work addict, I
have to confess having occasionally envied the guy who knows
how to be "lazy." This is the person for whom being carefree is
properly related to rest, to Sabbath. He knows how to stretch
unambitiously, naturally grasping the art of relaxing. Relaxation
need not be *irresponsible* laziness—wasting time that will not
yield a positive return. What God *commands* is rejuvenating
times of peaceful serenity. The English word *lazy*, in one of its

connotations, means relaxed, slow-moving, as in delicious expressions like *a lazy summer day* or *a lazy, drifting river*. A depressed person does not experience this kind of restorative, therapeutic inactivity. The ability to unwind, to rest, is a *healthful* virtue, ordained by God in the fourth commandment.

More Than Just a Deadly Sin

It seems cruel to dismiss depression as nothing but a deadly sin. The reductionism implied in the phrase "nothing but" is more characteristic of secularist philosophy than of the Christian view of psychological phenomena. Deeply insightful Christian writers have seen rich complexity in most of life's difficulties; it is the atheist who tries to reduce all life's intricacies to chemical reactions. We are not encouraged by Scripture or ancient theologians to reduce sloth/depression to "nothing but" chemistry, even though biochemical abnormalities are characteristic. Take a careful look at the self-talk and actions of slothful/depressed people, and you will see that most depression includes sin and misbeliefs as part of the picture as well.

Amelia

Amelia's experience might help to illustrate this. At forty-eight, she loved her garden as much as she had twenty years earlier when she began to coax living things from the soil. Her kids were teenagers now, and petunias, begonias, roses, daisies, and marigolds became her babies—babies whose multicolored blooms set off a display resembling that of a Fourth of July skyrocket. She could never decide what she delighted in most: gazing at the radiant glow of brilliant hues at the hour of sunset, spending the morning hours with her hands in the rich, moist, blended soil, or taking deep draughts of the cool air, so purifying, so elemental, so "down to earth." Gardening had never failed to lift her spirits to wondrous thoughts of her Father in heaven—Creator, Originator, Gardener extraordinaire! Not that gardening was all she did. Oh, no. She was a vital, active person whose enthusiastic smile infected others with cheer. Devoted to her family, loving, pouring herself out in service to others, she had succeeded in reaching her life's goals.

That is, until two months ago, when her heart was broken. Suddenly her life was, she told herself, utterly ruined. Michael had left her for a woman half her age and twice as firm and smooth. She now saw her entire life, once so solid and meaningful, as an empty waste, a balloon with nothing in it but air. What was left? Nothing. Nothing mattered. There was nothing to do but sit in the kitchen and stare at the wall. The mornings, once fresh harbingers of glorious new days, were now only preludes to the slow, drawn-out hours dragging on to blessed darkness, the welcome close of another day. She fed the children mostly from cans. Without Michael, there was no more reason to cook than to do anything else. She looked occasionally at the vacuum cleaner but seldom brought herself to plug it in. When her eye fell on her quilting pattern, lying neglected on an end table, she turned away. How could she ever have cared for quilting?

Sleep? She hardly knew what it was, spending the dark hours in bed thinking of ways to end the drab tedium of what she now saw as a prison sentence, an interminable bondage to an existence not worth having. She was filled with heaviness. Her garden? She would never touch it again—why bother? For her efforts had been pointless, and the sight of her flowers and shrubs now made her gag. There was no comfort in religion. What good was faith? It only kindled angry thoughts of God the Designer, who had fabricated her only so He could watch her suffer. Prayers? No. She hadn't prayed for weeks. There was no sense trying to propel her leaden words all the way to a distant, uncaring deity.

I let her tell me all this, resonating in myself with her sense of helplessness. I had often felt along with my slothful/depressed clients their heaviness and the feelings of helplessness—so characteristic of clinical depression. It becomes difficult to believe that the sufferer is wrong, that she is full of misbeliefs, that her thoughts and words are lies of the devil, the world, and the flesh. Yet contrary to what she is now telling herself, *there is hope, her life is not pointless, and she can be lifted out of the pit.*

She is clearly suffering. Can this thing afflicting her be a deadly sin, the phenomenon called sloth by ancient theologians? Or is it all just disordered biochemistry? There is no question that a biochemical disorder is involved; this patient is ill. But is that all there is to depression? Could sin be involved as well? If believing the lies of the enemy when one has been given full knowledge of the truth is sin, then certainly Amelia was sinning. If insisting on her own worthlessness, the pointlessness and hopelessness of life, and sometimes the outright denial of God's goodness is not sin, what word would fairly describe it?

Because they saw the sin involved in sloth, the observations of Evagrius and John Cassian were more astute than those of secular science, which insists that it's not important (if relevant at all) to look at moral and spiritual reality. These two ancient Christian teachers described what they saw as a deadly sin *and* a sickness. They were right on. In this condition, sin and sickness combine to become a particularly ugly example of demonic evildoing.

I wanted to get down to the task of rooting out the evil, erroneous self-talk, if only Amelia would summon the will to work at it with me. But first, I put my compassionate feelings into words: "It must be a terrible shock to discover that Michael has left you for someone else after you have given your best to your marriage for all these years. You must be feeling enormous pain. But are you certain Michael is lost? You're sure he won't come back?"

"I don't know," she answered listlessly. "Why should he? And even if he came back, what would we have? Nothing! Nothing! There's nothing left. How would I ever trust him again?"

"It would be difficult, maybe impossible, to trust Michael completely," I admitted. "But it is possible to have a good marriage without immediately trusting your husband. Trust must be rebuilt over time. You would both have to work at repairing the breech. Yet it *can* be done. And most often, adulterous relationships like the one Michael is involved in don't survive. It's very likely that he and his unfortunate choice will become very tired of each other and that Michael will want to come home to you."

"I don't think I could ever take him back. It's just too hard. Besides, I don't think he will try. He's never been one to humble himself to anybody. I don't see any chance for us now. Everything is down the drain."

"You've lost *everything*? How do you figure? Let's assume he *has* gone for good. How have you lost everything?"

"Everything worth having, yes. He was my whole life. I can't go on without him."

"The kids? Your ministries at church? What about God? Isn't He still there?"

"I don't know."

"Have you been praying?"

"Not really. My prayers don't work anyway. I used to pray every day. I tried so hard. What good did it do? God doesn't listen to me—if there is a God . . ."

"What do you think God would say to you right now?"

"I don't know. Not much. He never says anything to me. What do you think He would say?"

"I think God would say, 'Perhaps Michael *is* gone forever. You can't be certain about that. But you can be certain of My love and of My promise that I will put things right. You still have *Me*. Nothing has changed between you and Me. My promise to see you through is still sure. And meanwhile your problem now is not your loss but sickness and sin. Your task is to get over the illness and repent of the sin, to get back to the things I have called you to be and do. You can get over this.' That is what I believe God is saying to you right now. Are you willing to work at getting better? I'll stick with you and help you, but I need to know you are willing to try."

"Try? How? I can't make things change, whatever I do. Besides, I don't think I can do much right now. I can't even cook, so how can I make things better?"

"Do you really want to know how to make things better?"

"I guess so."

"Will you work at it?"

"Yes, I suppose."

"All right. You are saying that without Michael your life is over. Aren't you telling yourself you can never be happy and fulfilled again, no matter what, because he was your whole life?"

"Well, he was. I've been miserable ever since he told me he was leaving."

"Wouldn't anybody who is certain, as you are, that life is over be miserable? Wouldn't she be constantly convincing herself that she can't be anything or do anything but feel wretched?"

"Yes."

"So if there is no hope for you, if your self-talk is true, you have no reason ever to get better, right? But what if this notion is untrue? What if it is a warping of God's own Word to you? What if experience shows that you *can* get better? Then you might have a reason. Do you agree?"

"Uh-huh, *if* these thoughts are false, as you say they are."

"Well, let's look at your contention. You are telling yourself you have to be miserable because without Michael your life is hopeless. But consider this: Was there ever a time in your life when you didn't have Michael? When you didn't even know him?"

"Well, sure. What a question!"

"When you didn't have Michael, didn't even know him yet, were you ever happy and fulfilled?"

"Of course. I was very active and popular in school and just generally a happy person."

"Without Michael?"

"Okay, I see what you're driving at. Maybe I've been wrong about that. But—"

"Then why not stop telling yourself your life is over and the future is hopeless because Michael isn't around right now? Yes, your heart is in pain because you love Michael and because you trusted him. But is your faith in God's promises—His love, His goodness, His mercy, His faithfulness—or is it in Michael? God is whispering in your ear that pain and joy are not mutually exclusive. He wants you to know that He is no less present at this time than at any other. He can and will take the mess made by human sinfulness and utilize it for His glory. Your joy will come not from avoiding all difficulty and choosing numbness, but rather from embracing God's will for you, from believing what is true, and from recognizing that it is in eternity that every tear, every ache, every sadness, every evil will be removed."

"You really think my heart can change?"

Amelia began at this point to see a tiny sliver of light. As we worked together to find the way out of despair and into the bright light of hope, as she learned she could choose to get out of the morass of depression, we had some major tasks to accomplish. I told her about (1) *the principle of checking internal speech and replacing the misbeliefs of depression with the truth,* (2) *the principle of choosing incompatible behavior,* and (3) *the principle of making moral choices with zealous determination.* (See chapter 1.)

First of all, it was important, as it is with any depression, to get her *will* activated. Depressed people typically tell themselves they can't do things—simple things like Amelia's daily tasks of cooking and caring for her children. Persuading her to follow through on those—which was incompatible with her slothful inactivity—and to do so with zealous determination, *did* cause her to stop believing she was helpless. Rooting out her misbeliefs and replacing them with truth gradually overcame Amelia's belief that she couldn't help preaching false, God-denying thoughts and beliefs to herself. In addition to her being willing to work at all this, her physician prescribed an antidepressant. She began to feel better in about two weeks, much better in three. We continued our work together for another month after Amelia was back to normal in her feelings, her self-talk, and her activities.

Michael came home. Devastated in realizing what he had done, he wanted to repent of his sin and to love his wife and children. With the help of God, Amelia and Michael did reconcile, and they rededicated themselves to God and to one another. Though healing was not immediate, instantaneous, or pain-free, the light defeated the darkness, and depression was vanquished.

Painful Sickness Teamed Up With Deadly Sin

Sloth hurts. Yes, *all* sin eventually brings painful consequences in its wake. But unlike the other sins, with the exception of envy, the sin of sloth *itself* involves mild-to-severe levels of subjective distress. This has led many writers and most clinicians to emphasize the slothful person's anguished feelings. Both Aldous Huxley and T. S. Eliot have conjectured that acedia might be the medieval forerunner of modern *melancholy, ennui,* and *Weltschmerz.*[12]

Perhaps because of the picture of suffering presented by the slothful, there has been a tendency from the beginning to see in acedia some of the characteristics of a disease. As Cassian indicated, as early a writer as Evagrius, for instance, attributed the sin to the attack of an external agent, specifically to the onslaught of "the noonday demon" of Psalm 91:6.[13] This conception of being attacked by an outside perpetrator parallels the disease notion. In fact, some scholastics anticipated today's commonly held opinion that the cause of depression is to be found in disturbed brain chemistry. They attributed acedia to an imbalance of humors ("humors" were thought to be similar to what we know as chemicals). John of Wales and others suggested acedia might be caused or aggravated by a physiological defect.[14] Roger Bacon suggested that for some the remedy might be "recreation rather than resolution."[15]

Some slothful people even sense that something may be physically wrong, and they are usually correct. Among other characteristics, an element in most cases of depression is disordered biochemistry, a condition in which some neurotransmitting[16] chemicals like serotonin and norepinephrine are not available to nerve cells in adequate amounts. This situation in the brain brings with it a depletion of energy, feelings of mental, physical, and emotional heaviness, and a sense that it is pointless to make an effort to do things—especially projects that carry some risk, like astutely investing your boss's money.[17]

About 60 to 75 percent of depressed patients respond, to some extent, to antidepressant medication. Does this prove that all depression is caused by chemicals? Not at all. A significant minority of people *do not* respond to medication, a majority of depressed patients do respond well to psychotherapy *without* medication, and a very small number of severe intractable depressives do not respond to either. (Eighty percent of these respond to electroshock therapy.)

Low Spiritual Energy and Unresponsiveness to God

As previously mentioned, the sadness and apathy of the slothful occur "in the face of spiritual good," against God's goodness. This is the phenomenon of unresponsiveness to God and His gracious promises—the remarkable lack of spiritual energy exhibited by Amelia. If you have tried consoling a person suffering with acedia, you have seen that it's common for them to speak of being unable to make contact with God or of indifference in worship and prayer. It seems, however, that this failure to find spiritual effort rewarding is of a piece with the overall listlessness and apathy of the slothful. For them *every* kind of effort is too great, and most life experiences seem too lackluster and aversive.

It is important to notice the *subjective* sense of helplessness described by the slothful. This is the reason for the observation that this disposition is a disease, a demon, or a weakness and impairment of some faculty—especially the will. The slothful tend to say, "I cannot" where others would say, "I will not."

In full awareness of the sadness and seeming helplessness of people in the throes of sloth, moral theologians, whom Evelyn Waugh[18] has called "the least rhetorical of writers," condemn the untruthful self-talk and the refusal to exert effort as sin. "Sin" is not employed merely as a striking expression, says Waugh. Choice and responsibility are implied. Inactivity is a choice, as is a lackadaisical response to spiritual good, together with the torpor and tepidity that accompany it. Self-talk is a choice as well, and it may be changed by sustained effort of the will. These writers insist that *choices* are in part made by the slothful, even if only by default. The implication in the choice of the word *sin* is that *one can choose otherwise.*

No doubt it comes as a shock to us today that Christians of old were taught to see what we call depression as sin. *Sin implies responsibility and failure to carry out our duties.* But because the thought climate of our time places so much emphasis on individual subjective feelings and so little emphasis on individual moral decisions, we have emphasized the grief and sorrow elements of depression and have given little attention to the vice. Therefore we call it illness (which it is, in part, but only in part) and depend on medications such as Elavil, Paxil, and Prozac or on psychotherapy (all of which are effective when appropriate) to deal with it. The notions that using our will, making moral decisions, changing untruthful self-talk, doing things we don't feel like doing, and exerting effort we don't feel we can make might never be mentioned. Thus, the slothful soul drifts along in habits of sin, convinced that he has no willpower or that he need not exert his will when he can feel better by taking a pill.[19] One writer's verbal caricature of the slothful person states that she "lies down full length on life as though it were a sickbed."[20]

Which category is the correct one—is sloth a sickness or a sin? There are only three practical options: (1) Sloth is an illness; (2) Sloth is a sin; or (3) Sloth is a complex mixture of sin and sickness. In view of the spiritual, theological, and scientific evidence, the most accurate summary is the third option. Those who cannot bring themselves to believe that a sinful element is present should attend to the triad of misbeliefs routinely found in the self-talk of the depressed: devaluation of the self, of daily life, and of the future. The violation of truth involved in these themes, asserted by individuals who once knew them to be false, must be considered sinful.

I believe sloth is what we now call clinical depression. And I believe that sloth/depression *involves* biochemical brain changes that are effectively and routinely treated with antidepressant medication and/or psychotherapy. What is often lacking in contemporary approaches is therapy directed at activating the sufferer's will and therefore activating her own effort to stop saying,

"I can't" and begin saying, "I *will* through Christ who strengthens me."

Sloth in the Sin Test

You might be interested now in responding to some of the Sloth Scale items of the Sin Test. Answer True or False.

___F___   1. Often I feel worthless.

___F___   2. Often I feel just too tired or weak to do much of anything.

___F___   3. Much of the time I feel hopeless about life.

___T___   4. My conscience often bothers me with the feeling that I am not doing what I ought to be doing.

___F___   5. Sometimes I feel as though nothing in life seems really worth doing.

___F___   6. When I want to have a good time I would rather sit around drinking with a congenial group of friends than do something active.

___F___   7. I often get to the point where I feel like quitting and must just force myself to keep going.

___T___   8. I seldom have plenty of energy.

___F___   9. Much of the time I am angry with myself.

___F___   10. I often feel low-spirited and sad.

To score, simply count all the items you answered True.

Examine Your Understanding of Sloth

---

1. What psychological diagnosis is highly correlated with sloth and very much resembles this deadly sin?

2. How is sloth described in Isaiah 61:3 (KJV)? As a "spirit of _____."

3. Name at least three of the elements that may be found in sloth.

4. What does it mean that sloth is a "genuinely *theological* sin"?

5. What bad effect may sloth have on our relations with God?

For Further Thought and Discussion

1. If sloth is the same thing as depression, depression is one of the Deadly Sins. Should we then tell people who want help to go home and shape up—that they are feeling sorry for themselves, just full of self-pity?

2. You are discussing the issue of sloth and whether or not depression is sinful. You are arguing that depression might very well be a deadly sin. The other person says, "Religion should stay out of this. It's a medical issue entirely. What did Evagrius, Cassian, or Aquinas know about psychiatry? I think our new knowledge disqualifies such out-of-date sources." How would you respond?

3. Can you properly equate sloth and laziness? Why? Why not?

4. How can we adequately classify a condition that is both sickness and sin? Are there any other conditions like this? Alcoholism, for instance?

5. What do you think is the spiritual condition of a person who, in the throes of sloth/depression, states that God does not care about him? Has he lost his faith? Is he so sick he can't be held responsible for his words and deeds? What would you say to start him on the road to recovery?

Notes

1. John Cassian, *The Twelve Books on the Institutes of the Coenobia and the Remedies for the Eight Principal Faults*, chapter I. http://www.osb.org/lectio/cassian/inst/index.html.
2. Evagrius of Pontus (345–399) was one of the elders living the monastic life in the desert. John Cassian seems to have learned much about the Deadly Sins from Evagrius.
3. The Septuagint is the standard Greek translation of the Hebrew Old Testament. Many of the New Testament citations of Old Testament references are taken from the Septuagint.
4. William F. May, *A Catalogue of Sins: A Contemporary Exami-

nation of Christian Conscience (New York: Holt, Rinehart, and Winston, 1967), 195.

5. Ca. A.D. 730

6. Op. cit.

7. Siegfried Wenzel, *The Sin of Sloth: "Accedia" in Medieval Thought and Literature* (Chapel Hill, N.C.: University of North Carolina Press, 1967), 53.

8. From Cassian, cited in Wenzel, 19, 21.

9. From Adam Scot, cited in Wenzel, 33.

10. Born in A.D. 776 and archbishop of Mainz from 847–856, Maurus was a Benedictine scholar who left a substantial body of work, including biblical commentaries and many Latin poems.

11. A feature article on electroshock therapy for severe, intractable depression concludes with this interesting note: "It is popular to assume that all emotional and mental problems can be reduced to their molecular level . . . and be treated in a physical way. But that may be oversimplified. We are avoiding some interesting questions. If it's just biological, why has [mental illness] risen so dramatically in our culture? Can our thoughts, or life itself, be the cause of our mental illness? Can our behavior be the cause of mental illness? And if your behavior and thoughts make you ill, can't they also make you well?" (Josephine Marcotty, *Minneapolis StarTribune*, November 17, 1999, A16).

12. Aldous Huxley, Accidie, in *On the Margin: Notes and Essays* (London: n.p., 1923), 18–25, and T. S. Eliot, Baudelaire, in *Selected Essays, 1917–1932* (New York: n.p., 1932), 339. Both cited in Wenzel, 127. *Ennui* is a French word meaning "boredom." *Weltschmerz* is a German word meaning, literally, "world pain." The idea of Weltschmerz is one of pessimism evoked by the world; it may be roughly equivalent to the word "vanity" in Ecclesiastes.

13. In the Latin translation used by Evagrius, the word for "destruction" is translated "demon."

14. Wenzel, 59.

15. Moralis Philosophia, III, vii, 8, 181, cited in Wenzel, 59–60.

16. Neurotransmitters are chemical compounds generated in the body. Their function in alleviating sloth is to facilitate transmission of nerve impulses in the brain.

17. Matthew 25:26
18. Evelyn Waugh, Sloth, in Angus Wilson, et al., *The Seven Deadly Sins* (New York: William Morrow, 1962), n.p.
19. I hope it is clear that I am not knocking medication for sloth/ depression. I am only urging that we include a consideration of the sin involved in the complex picture presented by this syndrome.
20. Anonymous tract, *The Seven Capital Sins*, 1959, 47.

Chapter 7

Lust—What It Promises and What It Delivers

Lust and gluttony, related as they are to robust, repeatable delight, do not lose the attractiveness and allure of sex and gastronomy merely because they can become preoccupations until, at some point, they shade over into deadly sins. Likewise, we do not readily catch on to what is happening, so slow are we to view our own pleasures as having gotten out of hand and wicked. It is precisely the genuinely delightful that wears the mantle of evil most awkwardly. And what promises more delights than the vouchers handed out by lust?

Not for nothing has lust been called "our national sin." Whether or not lust has earned this reputation, it's surely in the running for the title. Writers, producers, performers, and musicians call the shots, determining what will be presented to us. They insist that they are only catering to public demands, but there is good reason to question this defensive maneuver. Entertainers, movie moguls, and the TV/print media are currently steering our cultural inclinations toward a zero-restraint level. In large numbers, those who have made it to the "top" preach the doctrine that man has no great need for God or His truth. Besides, they say, even if He exists, He must be a "good guy" who has nothing against us doing what we want to do. On matters of sex, most people seem bound to hold at least *some* tenets of a peculiar sort of secular orthodoxy.

The Secular Doctrine of Sex

The world's view of sex amounts to a catechism of beliefs at odds with human welfare and the social institutions devised to support it. This orthodox creed includes two major teachings. First, that sex is an instrumental good, not an intrinsic good. This means that sex is not valued for what it is but rather for the sake of what it gives us; it is an *instrument* for getting pleasure or feelings of closeness or offspring or some other goal of the autonomous individual. Second, that so long as the sex act is consensual, it cannot be considered immoral or harmful. Conformity to this creed is becoming obligatory, as in Aldous Huxley's novel, *Brave New World*, where "Everybody belongs to everybody else" is a slogan taught in school.

St. Augustine and St. Thomas Aquinas noticed a phenomenon that has become obvious to anyone observing the contemporary scene: "Man cannot live without joy; therefore when he is deprived of true spiritual joys it is necessary that he become addicted to carnal pleasures."[1] According to this insight, sex rushes in to fill the empty space when God has been expelled. Although sexual expression without any boundaries has not yet become *de rigueur*, the belief that sex is good simply because it is pleasurable—and that it is morally right as long as the participants are consenting—is widely enunciated in so many words. It is becoming the banner of our culture.

The entertainment industry can be very persuasive: A large part of the public now thinks that what was once considered sinful lust is actually innocent fun. Hedonism is preached by glitzy teen-centered sitcoms and dramas as well as by those such as Geraldo Rivera and Jerry Springer, purveying their own "wisdom" regarding the sexual spirit of the age and the sexual behavior of celebrities in high places. But the problem is *not* that sex is everywhere. Christianity has absolutely no objection to sex; in fact, it is clear to believers that God created sex as an *intrinsic* good. It's the perverted *secular doctrine* of sex that is unacceptable, not only to Christians but also to many non-Christians who maintain a rational and consistent ethic.

Sometime in the not too distant past, the Christian understanding that lust is a deadly sin, a vice that can destroy you, was labeled a relic almost as odd-sounding as the ridiculous notion that women don't have souls or that the earth is flat. More recently, especially because of its opposition to *unnatural* lust, the scriptural view of sex has ceased to amuse and has begun to get on the nerves of those who can hardly wait for secularism to direct everybody's actions all the time. In fact, even now, outright persecution occasionally awaits people who courageously oppose sexual sin. It is widely and earnestly declared that advocates of traditional morality should keep their opinions to themselves because the utterance of such strictures is unduly burdensome to others.

The facts confirm the teaching of God's Word about human sexuality. The Bible's moral truth is not a burden; it is a gift of God aimed at human wholeness and well-being. By discarding these important precepts, educators and the media have warped and disfigured God's design, altering sexuality itself so that it is no longer an enrapturing mystery but a dull duty one had better perform if one is to be considered normal. The life of a child reared without a father in the home, the marginal existence of a single mother on welfare, the agony of an AIDS patient, the symptoms of various other diseases contracted through sexual intercourse—all the consequences of lustful behavior—confirm for commonsense thinkers the desirability of the biblical standard of purity.

In many quarters, the unexpected has happened. For the jaded, the thrill of heterosexual intercourse has worn off. What used to be incredibly exciting has become the victim of monotony from "too much, too easy." With persistent irrationality, in spite of repeated research results to the contrary, regular sex is often said to be dull, boring, and unsatisfying. Replacing it on the titillating brink of the forbidden are variants and perversions like homosexuality, sadomasochism, bestiality, and now, with the encouragement of the American Psychological Association, adult/child couplings, both homosexual and heterosexual. For most of us such practices are nauseating, but that's all right with those who promote them. Do you know why? Because in matters of lust there is a slippery slope. If you look at the examples of countries considered to be even more permissive than the United States, you'll note that with the enthusiastic promotion of entertainment and news media, illicit practices move quickly from unthinkable to thinkable to interesting to acceptable and finally from acceptable to codification into law.

A Stunning Prophecy Fulfilled

A close-to-home example of this phenomenon can be found in the reaction to a prophecy given by David Wilkerson in the early 1970s at the Lutheran Conference on the Holy Spirit in Minneapolis. Homosexuality, Wilkerson foretold, will soon become commonplace and widely accepted. Churches will pronounce same-sex coupling as morally acceptable, and ordained homosexual clergy will bless homosexual marriages. "No way," many of us said. "This will never happen." If the speaker hadn't been David Wilkerson, most of us would have said, with confidence, "He is out of his mind." Yet his prophetic "batting average" was so remarkable that we listened respectfully to what seemed incredible.

Not so many years later, just look at what has happened. The "correct" word is now "gay." Both the American Psychiatric Association and the American Psychological Association have officially removed homosexuality from their diagnostic manual of behavioral disorders, thus declaring it perfectly normal. This action is based not on new knowledge or research but on unvarnished political arm-twisting. The Evangelical Lutheran Church in America now encourages a rethinking of the biblical teachings about same-sex coupling and other kinds of extramarital sexual behavior. I reiterate that all of this has been accomplished, not by empirical research on human sexuality, not by new light on any passages of Scripture, but merely by repeatedly exposing the clergy and laity to falsehoods and political pressure. In psychology this process of gradual exposure is called "systematic desensitization." We do not readily accept the unmentionable until we are numbed by repetition. After the unmentionable has been mentioned often enough, it becomes mentionable but still undoable. Yet after the undoable is done routinely, we begin to have a hard time accepting the idea that it is evil and must therefore be given up.

Lustful Behavior Identified

The case against illicit pleasure usually smacks of the killjoy and the spoilsport, especially when the issue is lust. The argument against lust is perceived to have been weakened by writers (some with a vested interest in deviance) such as the Marquis de Sade, Havelock Ellis, Sigmund Freud, and the twisted distorter, Alfred Kinsey. It turns out that all of them got their data wrong, and that Kinsey, for example, was writing in the service not of objectively gathered facts but of his own perversions. Now, in a society where Larry Flynt has become an expert on morality, it's difficult to find many people who care.

Charles Krauthammer has described the way we moralists come off: "Bluenoses demand restraint against the porn and violence that are the staple of popular culture." Facts have always had a hard time standing up to appetite. So to the person committing fornication or adultery, his sin *appears* to be the same innocent love, the same tender delight in the other that marriage offers to couples who choose it. This may be the reason for Augustine's statement that he found it impossible to convince adulterers that they were in mortal sin.[2]

Advocates of lust plead their case. How could committed relationships between the unmarried be sinful? They don't harm anyone, especially since we have effective contraceptives and legal abortion to prevent unwanted children from coming into the world. So nobody is hurt, right?

Wrong. Absolutely wrong. Sexual sin is roundly condemned

by Jesus. He makes Dr. Laura look like a libertine by comparison, for He radically redefines lust as more than illicit *action*. His definition begins with fantasizing—mental rehearsal of the wicked behavior (Matthew 5:27–28). Many sins first occur in the mind but none more pleasurably than lust. This sin, when practiced in the imagination, is capable of eliciting physical arousal and of paving the way from mental pictures to overt behavior.

Lustful behavior includes adultery, fornication (sex outside marriage), use of pornography, perversion (homosexuality, pedophilia, bestiality, sadism, masochism, voyeurism, exhibitionism, and the like), or fantasizing any of this. It's hard to manage the vocabulary related to varieties of sexual sin because of the rapid change in language over the past thirty or so years. Lust is the vice opposed to the virtue of chastity. Not celibacy—*chastity*. It is a vice because it violates both the intention and the commandment of the Creator who invented sex.

Lust Begins in the Mind

The word *lust* has changed in its implications, for many people no longer consider it bad. Some individuals who took the Sin Test were very proud of their high lust scores because they thought of it as a positive, desirable attribute, like muscle mass or IQ. But no matter how acceptable lust may be among your peers, it has not changed its status: It's a deadly sin. The English word *lust* means intense or unrestrained sexual craving. Derivatively it also can mean intense craving for other things, such as power. As a matter of fact, lust begins in the mind. Samuel Smiles wrote:

> Sow a thought, reap an act.
> Sow an act, reap a habit.
> Sow a habit, reap a character.
> Sow a character, reap a destiny.[3]

Why Change for the Better is Difficult

Treatment for sexual sins can be a tremendous challenge, especially in view of three widespread societal trends. First, *shame is out.* In an earlier age and culture, women were raised with the clear realization that they could ruin their lives by becoming pregnant out of wedlock, since they would be shamed by society. Today this concept has been destroyed, replaced by the radical notion that women ought to enjoy sexual adventures because they are or should be exactly like men. The insistence by females on marriage as a condition for sex, making premarital sex less likely, has been eradicated. Now it is shaming itself that has become shameful. With little feminine resistance to illicit sex, it's quite easy for a determined male to find a willing partner free of charge.

Second, *people have faith in "safe sex."* This is the false notion that condoms and other contraceptives remove the hazards involved in sexual sin by preventing disease and conception. However, the effectiveness of such devices is limited. They are not failure-proof against either pregnancy or sexually transmitted diseases, including AIDS. But since this is rarely made clear, it's difficult for some to believe that what they are doing is wrong or harmful. It may occur only slowly even to some Christians that they must change their behavior if they want to repent and walk in the light as Christ Jesus is in the light (1 John 1:6–7).

Third, *pornography is so readily available.* Habits that bring sexual satisfaction, no matter how perverse, are powerfully reinforced by repetition. Today, pornography is easily accessible without the fear of being caught and embarrassed or humiliated by a shopping trip to a stigmatized bookstore; such hindrances are now irrelevant. The nearby video outlet or the nearest magazine counter can supply plenty of material. It isn't even necessary to find a partner in order to enjoy sex if one is immersed in internet pornography or X-rated movies on pay-per-view TV. The passage is more true than ever: *The righteousness of the upright delivers them, but the treacherous are taken captive by their lust* (Proverbs 11:6).

An interesting term occurs in Ephesians 4: "deceitful lusts." The peculiar ability of lust to deceive us appears in everyday life as we mentally rehearse some forbidden sexual pleasure. This is called fantasizing, and many have observed that sexual fantasy can be so "fantastic" as to make the reality disappointing. Fantasy amounts to misbelief, for it eliminates the truth about evil behavior and especially its dreadful consequences. Ephesians 4:22–24 orders us to forsake this disastrous pursuit:

> Put off your old nature which belongs to your former manner of life and is corrupt through deceitful lusts (*epithumia*), and be renewed in the spirit of your minds, and put on the new nature, created after the likeness of God in true righteousness and holiness.

I realize that most people have only a vague notion of the place of sin in the mix of pathologies presented by clients to their counselors. Many professionals believe sin need not be discussed at all, that the exploration of the human soul must be a secular-scientific enterprise, and that sexual behavior can be treated as morally neutral. I am also aware that some readers agree that psychology is one thing and moral considerations an entirely different thing, especially when it comes to sex. I have tried, so far as possible without revealing any client's identity, to make the Seven Deadly Sins as serious a concern to you, my reader, as they have become to me. But for some, lust poses a special problem, partly because powerful cultural forces have made war against the notion that lust is sinful. While some popular plays, sitcoms, movies, and books have presented stories exposing the ugly consequences of pride, envy, and other deadly sins, the arts have frequently pictured loose sexual morals as affording nothing but pleasure. All in all, the mass media have done better at presenting lust as harmless amusement than at telling the truth about its power to destroy lives. The illusion that illicit sex is unbridled fun, undiluted enjoyment, with no cost and no consequences, the fable that immoral coupling exacts no penalties, couldn't portray the results of lust less accurately.

From my vantage point as a clinician, the deadly sin of lust brings innumerable ugly consequences in its wake, including pain, anguish, poverty, ignorance, bigotry, sickness, mental illness, and even death, as well as the huge economic costs they generate. Like most psychologists, I have seen many clients who desired help with depression, anxiety, and guilt attached in some way to lust—their own or someone else's lustful behavior. Most were males. Some were fathers or stepfathers who molested their children; some were men who lured little boys into their homes to involve them in sex play;[4] some were men who exposed themselves to women in public, or men who roamed around at night looking through bedroom windows to gaze at women taking their clothes off; some, occasionally, were men who habitually molested total strangers. Few of these men came for help until they were charged with a crime and a judge ordered treatment as a condition of probation. Some sought help with their struggles against pornography, and one or two presented bizarre attractions to animals or objects (like shoes, feet, or underwear). A few were married women entrapped in their own adultery. A few were young, unmarried, exceptionally pretty girls like Colleen, whose malady was deep self-abhorrence correlated with a conundrum she faced on almost every date. I remember Colleen for her anguished self-detestation.

Colleen

Did she have difficulty attracting men? No way. With her honey-colored hair, glowing complexion, and eyes of deep violet, getting male attention was not an issue for Colleen. Nearly all the available men she met wanted to date her. But the problem arose a little later. Not that Colleen was cold or rejecting. On the contrary, she gave herself freely to every man who made a pass at her, and then she hated herself for being cheap. Her relationships didn't last.

"I don't know why, but after one or two dates, after we have sex, guys don't call anymore. Even when I've tried calling them, they're suddenly busy or they want another turn in bed. Afterwards they leave."

"I imagine you've thought a lot about what might cause them to act this way. You've probably come up with some ideas of your own," I said, although I had a pretty fair guess as to what might be the answer.

She thought about this and then replied, slowly, "I don't know. Nothing I try works. All I want is a relationship with a future, but all the men I meet decide they don't want me after all—or they only want sex. I must be pretty uninteresting. I do try to talk on dates, but it hasn't helped. I've thought about going back to school. Maybe that would make me more attractive to men. I . . . I don't seem to have whatever it takes to hang on to a guy."

"So you've decided to get some help."

"I guess so. I don't even know if I've come to the right place. But I know I need something."

"What was it that tipped the scales and made you finally decide you needed to talk to someone about the situation?"

"The last guy I dated. He set a record! On our first date, he talked me into having sex with him, made me do some things I've never ever done before (I was desperate!). I hated it. Then afterwards he put on his clothes and left. We didn't even go out! It was a nightmare. I didn't want to do anything like we did. He was a yahoo. He wasn't attractive or sexy. He almost made me sick at my stomach. Anyway, I cried all that night, and I haven't been able to sleep very well since. Being dumped by a slob from the bottom of the heap proves I'm not what guys want. For some reason, nobody wants me. I'm so depressed."

"Have you ever asked any of these men what the problem was?"

"Only once. Never again. I said, 'I don't get it. You wanted sex, and after you got it you dumped me. What's the deal?' He said, 'Lady, I'm not the only one who wanted sex and got it, remember? And, hey, you didn't *buy* me by sleeping with me once, you know.' It was like a knife in my ribs. I never asked that question again. I couldn't handle any more of that sort of thing."

"I don't blame you. What a clod! Colleen, would you tell me a little bit about what goes through your mind when you're feeling hurt and depressed about this?"

"I think and think, *What could be wrong with me? Why am I such a reject?* I try to consider every angle, even maybe wearing perfume or getting a facelift, but I know men find me attractive—to begin with. I must be one of those people who looks fine, but I'm sure now I'm repulsive to men when they get to know me a little better. I don't know why. It's hopeless, I think."

"Could you please tell me your feelings about your sex life? Are you happy with it?"

"Are you kidding? I feel like a slut. I wish men didn't expect to have sex like they do, but that's the way guys are, I guess."

"Did it ever cross your mind that there might be desirable men out there who would think more highly of you if you turned them down? Didn't go to bed with them?"

"No, I don't think so. They all seem to expect it."

"Have you considered that the old wisdom about this might be correct? After all, you haven't dated everybody!"

"What do you mean?"

"By 'the old wisdom,' I mean a thing most women used to understand very well because their mothers and grandmothers made a point of telling them before they were old enough to spend time with men. Growing girls were taught that men who want long-term relationships want women who are not easy, women who are capable of saying no—so that, even though a man may make a bid for sex early in a relationship, he will stay around much longer if he finds someone who thinks enough of herself to refuse, to keep herself for marriage. I know the current mythology holds that free and easy sex is an essential ingredient in the single life, but maybe, just maybe, you and multitudes of other women have been swindled by that idea."

"I don't know. Everybody does it. I mean, all the guys I ever date expect to have sex, if not on the first date, they figure on getting it by the second or third time. I've tried to say no but I can't make it stick."

"So it's no wonder you assume there's no other way to go.

And I think you are correct about the guys you date. *Probably.* But not everyone is the same. Not every man expects to have sex before marriage. For example, Christian men who take their commitment to Christ seriously might be different, even though I can't guarantee that simply because you meet someone at a Christian social gathering, you can be certain he will have good morals. It's a probability thing. Did it ever occur to you that the likelihood of finding someone with strong ethics would be higher if you dated men from church? Or did you ever think of this: Even a man who tries to have sex with you early in the relationship could be assuming that you expect it and that if he doesn't try to get you to bed you'll think there's something wrong with him? Such a guy might be delighted to meet a woman who is warm, friendly, sincere, and determined to save sex for marriage."

"Gosh, no. That never crossed my mind. The men I date act like every girl does it, and if I don't, I'm an oddball. The message I get is that I'd never have any luck with men if I turned out to be a prude."

"Yet you end up despising yourself, telling yourself you're a slut. And that's part of what it's costing you to be like everybody else? That's the price you're willing to pay for not being called a prude?"

"I guess you're right. It is kind of like paying for a guy's approval."

"Here's what this looks like to me. You don't want to have sex with your dates, but you feel trapped, forced to go to bed with them in order to keep them interested. Right?"

"Yes. That's the way it is. I can't say no. It always ends up the same way when I try to refuse them. They beg, they get surly, I finally stop resisting, and pretty soon we're in bed."

"But as soon as they find out you're an easy mark, they seem to either want you for nothing but more sex or they drop you altogether and never call again. Have I understood you correctly so far?"

"Yeah, I get exactly nothing for giving them what they want."

"And meanwhile you feel terrible. Not only do you suffer rejection after you've given away a precious asset—yourself—but you despise yourself for being promiscuous. You feel awful about yourself and your status as nothing but an unpaid prostitute. Is this pretty accurate?"

"Oh, yes, it is. That's exactly how I feel."

Men picked up on Colleen's self-devaluation with uncanny speed, and they detected her sense of low self-worth because she communicated it without meaning to. Soon they moved on to other girls who were perhaps not so ready to prove their availability, leaving her to loathe herself still more. After all, no matter how readily she made her sexual favors available, men regularly abandoned her early in the game.

I suppose somewhere in the depths of her consciousness she knew that sex outside marriage was sinful lust, but she had concentrated on trying to please men and suppressed any thought of pleasing God and what might be His good and perfect will for her. Yet she had come to me specifically because she wanted a *Christian* psychologist. Did she consider herself a believer? Yes. How did she manage to square that with promiscuous sexual behavior? She allowed herself to think of what she did as not being sinful as long as she took precautions against pregnancy and disease. Had she ever studied the New Testament on the subject of fornication? No, but she said she was willing to if I thought it would help. I did, but she needed more than just prohibitions against sin.

"Why don't we make a plan that will, I'm pretty certain, make things very different," I suggested. "Are you willing to try some new behavior? Something more likely to lead to self-respect than what you have been doing?"

"That's why I'm here. I'll try whatever you suggest. But if you're going to tell me to quit going to bed with men, I'll probably end up an old maid for sure. I could try, but like I said, I never have managed to say no."

"All right, here is step one: You are to learn exactly what God's Word has to say about fornication." (It was Colleen's idea to do a concordance study of the words *lust* and *fornication* in the New Testament and to summarize what her findings revealed about God's will for her behavior. But to get back to our dialogue—)

"Step two: I will help you learn to say no regardless of what you think the consequences may be." She was far more enthusiastic about trying the plan than I had expected. I explained what I believed would happen. "You will probably find that some men will drop you if you don't sleep with them because their only interest is in getting free sex. You must ask yourself whether you really want to waste your time fighting such men off."

"I don't; I'm sick of those guys!" she replied with an emphatic sparkle in her eyes. She had already begun to sense the worth and value attached to being a discriminating daughter of the King rather than a commodity on the flesh market.

I continued. "What you will discover is that some men, the good ones among them, will be attracted to you precisely because you say no. They will value you because you value yourself and care about doing right and because you want to keep yourself for the man who will commit himself in marriage."

She was worried about being able to do what she had seldom had the courage to do before. "Can you really teach me to say no?" she asked.

"Yes, I can."

Colleen and I spent our next several sessions on refusal training. By modeling and rehearsing them, she learned new ways to verbalize her refusal to go to bed with dates—such as, "I like you a lot, but I don't know you very well, and I want to wait for marriage before I go to bed with anyone. For now, I would like to spend time together and maybe get better acquainted." I also taught her how to prevent and put a stop to improper touching and unwanted physical advances. We rehearsed appropriate speeches and actions until Colleen felt capable of doing them in the dating situation.

One day she opened our session with, "I went to a Christian singles group last weekend and a really cute guy asked for my phone number. I gave it to him. Is that all right?"

"Has he called you?"

"Not yet, but I think he will. Can I go out with him if he does call?"

"Sounds like a good opportunity to get to know someone who perhaps won't pressure you for sex. Unfortunately, even guys who attend Christian organizations can't be guaranteed pure. So you might have to use your new refusal skills with him. But, yes, I think it's time to put some of these things to the test. Remember, your reason for remaining pure will be to please God. If you aim at behaving like a child of God, you will be much more capable of success than if you keep your old aim of simply snagging a man. Yet a likely benefit of this change in attitude and approach will be that a good man will want to continue to get to know you, and even more important, you will respect yourself."

The original diagnosis for Colleen was *major depression* and *dependent personality disorder*. This makes sense because her dependency on men and the passive stance it generated led to her self-devaluating depression. But what is not contained in my psychological diagnosis is this: Her dependent passivity led to the deadly sin of lust. The sin was using sex—not to give herself to committed marriage and motherhood and family, but to obtain a man as a badge of worth for herself.

Incidentally, Colleen's is not a unique situation. Plenty of people engage in sexual behavior not, primarily, because they want to give in to lustful desires, but rather in order to "fit in." They choose sin in order to catch a mate who they expect will take care of their affectional needs forever and/or to prove to themselves that they are grown up and can actually cause a person of the opposite sex to want them.

Of course, Colleen's story has been altered and compressed for this book. An actual client whose case was somewhat similar to Colleen's saw me each week for about three months. Most of that time we spent modeling and rehearsing behavioral skills for her to use in coping with unwanted male sexual advances with tact and good humor.

Colleen's story, like most episodes illustrating trouble with lust, is gender-specific. Not often does it happen to men that they forfeit their chances with women by being willing to have sex. So when my editor, Christopher Soderstrom, asked me to include the story of a male parallel to Colleen's experience, I couldn't think of a precise analogy. Instead, what came to mind was a series of men who acted out their lust with serious consequences. For men, sex becomes a trap, a habit, an "addiction." Looked at from some people's perspective, women who indulge in illicit sex may seem to have much more to lose in consequence and that men only have something to gain. But in reality, what men have to gain may be a horrible habit that becomes a yoke around the neck. Instead of one case example of this sort of thing, a whole series of faces crowded into my mind:

Jorgen, a bank president, had played around with dirty pictures on the Internet until he discovered that even faced with his huge load of guilt, he was stuck. At first, like the typical alcoholic, he assured himself that he could and would stop clicking onto the smut pages. But he couldn't quit. Treatment for him was difficult and protracted.

Landon was hooked on his habit of visiting prostitutes on business trips. Haunted every time by the possibility that he, a respected businessman and president of his congregation, might be seen and recognized, he was full of fear. The anxiety—the very real threat of being caught—did not prevent his giving in, even though he stood to lose his family, his career, and his place of service in the fellowship of believers.

Marshall, caught in an affair with a woman in his own office, was torn nearly to pieces by the demands of his lover. She insisted that he get a divorce and marry her. He held the sure conviction that he did not want to lose his wife and children— but like many men he thought he couldn't give up the sin.

I think I may have written elsewhere of the couple whose tale of woe made me shudder and left me with absolutely no answer. "We both left our families, both divorced our spouses, and married each other. But our guilt is so horrendous, the love we thought was worth everything to us is turning to hate. What can we do?"

I recall another challenging case as well. Bobby was a politician who moved in a group of single political junkies, all of whom took sexual coupling for granted as a standard component of their social lives. But Bobby was in trouble. He had been experiencing impotence, maybe as a result of guilt, or fear of failure, or something organic. At any rate, there wasn't much room for all the delights lust had been promising him when he couldn't perform and he was sick with grief.

What is not usually understood these days is that people cannot utterly dismiss guilt and guilty feelings. Unlike the fantasy of secularism to the effect that sexual mores are simply prejudices we picked up in childhood, the reality is, according to Scripture and experience, that the law of God is written on our hearts. We can blur it but we cannot eradicate it. And indulging oneself in a test of the promises of lust will eventually bring drastic consequences—even for men (who often think they can easily get away with lustful behavior because they are guys and can't get pregnant). Such consequences can be horrific (including AIDS and even, in one case, the wreckage of an American presidency). Getting rid of these habits may require countermeasures such as changing your place of employment or altering your social life or moving your computer into the living room or traveling in pairs or accepting accountability.

In 1 Thessalonians 4:3–5 Paul illuminates our direction:

> For this is the will of God, your sanctification: that you abstain from unchastity (*porneia*); that each one of you know how to take a wife for himself in holiness and honor, not in the passion of lust (*epithumia*) like heathen who do not know God.

Second Peter 2:10 uses the second Greek word that is noted above as related to "those who indulge in the lust (epithumia) of defiling passion."

In a few passages, the secondary English meaning of the word *lust* occurs, meaning illicit desire for worldly thrills. First John 2:16–17 uses *lust* in the general sense of *inordinate evil desire for the things of the world.*

The Latin word used by the moral theologians for this deadly sin is usually *luxuria* (meaning "luxuriousness"). Why the fathers chose this term for lust I do not know. Other Latin words that could be used for the English word *lust* are *concupiscentia* and *libido*.

What to Do About Lust

Ask yourself, "How can I obey these serious injunctions from God? I know, if I am to be perfectly honest, that my spirit has been filled with the Holy Spirit. I am never left on my own, never sent to the cross to be forsaken by the Lord. And yet my sinful heart clings to thoughts that are impure, lustful, corrupt, unclean. What can I do? I can tell myself the truth about the whole reality of what I am doing. I can say to my mind and my will: 'Listen. There *is* another Voice of truth and purity. *Listen to it.* When He speaks, *obey it.* You are filled with the Spirit of truth, so listen to Him and obey Him.' " If you need help, admit it and get it. Don't stall, don't hide, don't turn away. Lust is not larger than God. Don't buy that lie.

Sin Test Results—Lust

According to the Sin Test, research subjects who had high scores on lust tended to have higher scores on MMPI Scale 4, which describes people who are more likely to entertain rebellious attitudes. This tendency is not necessarily evinced by illegal actions but more often by unconventionality, impulsivity, and a disposition to insist on immediate gratification for impulses and whims.

Lust Scale scores were also related to MMPI Scale 8, which describes an inclination to withdraw into oneself, focus on one's inner life, engage in daydreaming and fantasy, exhibit confusion, have difficulties in impulse control, and be troubled by fears, worries, and dissatisfactions.

In addition, scores on the Sin Test Lust Scale also appear related to scores on MMPI Scale 9. This scale tends to describe people having a high level of activity, a preference for action over careful thought, a wide range of interests, too many projects going at once, overly high self-appraisal, low frustration tolerance, unrealistic optimism, recurring irritability, and frequent angry outbursts. High 9s tend to prefer action to thought and tend to be energetic, talkative, easily bored, restless, outgoing, sociable, friendly, and enthusiastic. They may think that they are not getting enough out of life. Colleen's score on MMPI Scale 9 was greatly elevated.

Lust in the Sin Test

If you like, you can now test yourself on some of the Lust Scale items from the Sin Test. These items proved statistically to be among the most powerful for measuring the trait indicated by the Lust Scale. Answer True or False.

_F_ 1. Society has surrounded man's sex drive with too many prohibitions.

_F_ 2. Through long experience I have come to the conclusion that it's no use trying to fight sin.

_F_ 3. I especially enjoy watching movies depicting intimate love scenes.

_F_ 4. I think that sexual inhibitions are at the root of most people's problems.

_F_ 5. I think that any religion which teaches that God made man with a sex drive and then sets up so many restrictions around it is unreasonable.

_F_ 6. I don't care much for books or movies depicting a great deal of fighting or bloodshed.

_F_ 7. For some strange reason, I feel that forbidden sensual pleasures are more exciting and interesting than those which are not forbidden.

_F_ 8. No one can tell me when and how and with whom I can make love.

_F_ 9. If the people who have occupied themselves with ultimate problems like God and life after death had concentrated on the study of human sexual behavior and how to enrich it, the world would be a much better place today.

_ϝ_ 10. If I have a choice I will go to see a sexy movie in preference to most others.

Examine Your Understanding of Lust

1. How are lust and gluttony similar?

2. How are they different?

3. Which one is worse?

4. How does lust fail to keep its promises?

5. According to the dominant secular creed, is sex an instrumental good or an intrinsic good? Explain.

6. According to St. Augustine and St. Thomas Aquinas, sex rushes in to fill the void when _____ is expelled. Do you see their point?

7. Why did Colleen have difficulty keeping her relationships with men strong and healthy?

8. Why are sexual perversions becoming so widespread today? Why did the American Psychological Association remove homosexuality from its diagnostic manual of disorders?

For Further Thought and Discussion

1. What are the causes of the saturation of today's social climate with lust?

2. What should be done to reverse the current trend toward cultural acceptance (even enthusiastic endorsement) of lust?

3. Who (if anyone) ought to be doing more about this situation?

4. Have you noticed the gradual trend toward demonization of those who work to maintain a higher cultural standard regarding sexual issues?

5. What are your thoughts about the following argument concerning contraception (paraphrased from a Roman Catholic source)?

   Lust is the performing of the conjugal act with one's marriage partner exclusively for pleasure. The basis for this view of marital coitus (intercourse) is the Stoic doctrine of the natural law, incorporated in scholastic theology, and continued to the present day. The argument, roughly restated, derives the injunctions regulating the use of coitus from the "nature" of the act. Since coitus is the means of generating children, the purpose of the act must include generation. To engage in intercourse for pleasure only is to exclude part of the natural purpose of the act and therefore to violate the natural law. The dissent from this point of view by most non-Roman Catholics as well as by some within the ranks of current Roman Catholic thinkers is well known.

6. What do you think of the following arguments in response to the natural law argument against contraception? What is your opinion/belief about the morality of contraception?

   A. An argument from analogy. Eating sugar substitutes excludes one purpose of eating, which is to nourish. Is it a sin to eat sweets in moderation solely for pleasure? One purpose of sleeping is to renew one's physical reserves, but, that having been accomplished, is it a sin to sleep "in" for the pleasure of it?

B. An argument from logic. Major premise of above argument must be: "It is sinful to perform any natural act unless one includes (does not exclude) every part of the act's natural purpose." Can this premise be demonstrated from Scripture or reason?

C. An argument from Scripture. There would appear to be no doctrine of Scripture stating that the only natural purpose of the conjugal act is the begetting of children.

Notes

1. Cited in Peter Kreeft, *Back to Virtue* (San Francisco: Ignatius Press, 1992), 169.
2. Karl A. Olsson, *Seven Sins and Seven Virtues* (New York: Harper & Brothers, 1962), 58.
3. Ibid.
4. These people virtually never present themselves for treatment now. Since changes in the law require all counselors to report them to a government agency or the police, the threat of prosecution has become an effective barrier discouraging men who are troubled by their own evil behavior from seeking assistance.

Chapter 8

Gluttony—Selling Out to Pleasure

The deadly sins of lust and gluttony have many similarities. Each epitomizes the perversion of a God-invented source of enormous pleasure: sexual lovemaking and the taking of nourishment, respectively. We have distorted and promoted lust to fatten the entertainment industry, and we have made twisted, convoluted fun of gluttony. Sex and eating/drinking, when they are wrenched away from God's purposes, make us horribly vulnerable and exposed to spiritual attack. Why? Because in them so much of our animal nature champs at the bit, eager to join the war against the Spirit.

Moreover, lust and gluttony are especially the *hedonist's* sins, the hallmark failures of Søren Kierkegaard's aesthetic man in *Either/Or.*[1] As Kierkegaard viewed him, the hedonist-aesthete, serving his appetites with all his might and main, has not yet become a real human being because he has never once used his *will* to make a decision. Drifting along on the choppy ocean of his impulses, he has never made a commitment, nor has he any wish to do so. This is because by living entirely for pleasurable and comfortable feelings, he does what animals and natural man do instinctively.

The accomplished hedonist pursues pleasure with as much skill as she is able to muster and with as much gusto as she finds rewarding, but she has never dedicated herself to anything. Kierkegaard did his best, but none of his efforts to attack the fatally erroneous assumptions of gluttony by making the best possible case against them succeeded so convincingly as the aesthetic writings that argue brilliantly for the artful pursuit of pleasure. It's tough to make an attractive case *against* pleasure! So the great Christian visionary hoped that, by reading the best conceivable argument *for* the unceasing pursuit of pleasure, his hedonistic readers would see the bankruptcy of the soul traveling on that road—a road Kierkegaard knew led to damnation. It is also a road that soon leads to boredom, as you will discover when you later read the story of Tyler.

Clement's Portrait of Gluttony-Hedonism

Clement of Alexandria, in his *Instructor*, had success arguing against hedonism by drawing an unforgettably disgusting portrait of wanton gluttony. He writes of his fellow Alexandrians at banquets:

> How senseless to besmear their hands with condiments and to be constantly reaching to the sauce, cramming themselves immoderately and shamelessly, not like people tasting, but ravenously seizing! For you may see such people, liker swine or dogs for gluttony than men, in such a hurry to feed themselves full that both jaws are stuffed out at once, the veins about the face raised, and besides the perspiration running all over, as they are tightened with their insatiable greed.[2]

Clement offers his students clear and contrasting directions for appropriate behavior at table:

> We are to drink without contortion of the face, not greedily grasping the cup, nor before drinking making the eyes roll with unseemly motion; nor from intemperance are

we to drain the cup at a draught; nor besprinkling the chin, nor splash the garments with gulping down all the liquor at once—our face all but filling the bowl and drowning in it.[3]

The deadly sin of gluttony consists of an inordinate craving for the pleasures of eating and drinking or the same craving for something else. (The word inordinate once again brings Aristotle's Golden Mean to the forefront.) *Those pleasures, in themselves, are part of our biology.* They include the enjoyment of smell and flavor, the satisfied feeling caused by rising blood sugar, and the eradication of the pangs of hunger by the experience of fullness. *But pleasures must not be indulged to the ruination of the body, the neglect of duties, or the obscuring of God.* Stuffing oneself with quantities greater than nutrition demands is a violation of reason. We may have some questions about the validity of this approach when applied to such pleasures as marital sex, drinking a cup of coffee, or munching on a few M&M's. Yet clearly one who uses food or drink in such a way as to damage his health or to impair the faculties needed for him to function is guilty of gluttony. To eat or drink for the mere pleasure of the experience is likewise to commit the sin of gluttony.

Gross Gluttony

Typifying wanton gluttony, perhaps the most renowned appetite in history was the prodigious hunger of King Henry VIII (he of six wives and frequent resort to England's royal headsman to solve his marital difficulties). Henry consumed whole joints of meat together with liberal portions of fish and fowl at his daily banquet, in quantities astounding even to his contemporaries. But Henry was by no means the gluttonous exception to the rule in medieval Europe. It appears that the affluent may have regularly eaten in excess, devouring food and drink in massive quantities. Here is an example that comes from a late-fourteenth-century menu from *Menagier de Paris.*

FIRST COURSE
Miniature pastries filled either with cod liver or beef marrow

A cameline meat "brewet" (pieces of meat in a thin cinna-
  mon sauce)
Beef marrow fritters
Eels in a thick spicy puree
Loach (a freshwater fish) in a cold green sauce flavored with
  spices and sage
Large cuts of roast or boiled meat
Saltwater fish

SECOND COURSE
"The best roast that may be had"
Freshwater fish
Broth with bacon
A meat tile (pieces of chicken or veal, simmered, sautéed,
  served in a spiced sauce of pounded crayfish tails, al-
  monds, and toasted bread and garnished with whole
  crayfish tails)
Capon pasties (rhymes with "nasties") and crisps
Bream (a fish) and eel pasties
Blancmange (a flavored and sweetened milk pudding thick-
  ened with cornstarch)

THIRD COURSE
Frumenti (hulled wheat boiled in milk and flavored with
  sugar and spices)
Venison
Lampreys (like eel) and hot sauce
Fritters
Roast bream and darioles (a dish, as of vegetables, fish, cus-
  tard, or pastry, that is cooked and served in a small
  mold)
Sturgeon
Jellies

With each course, wine or ale was served. Manor houses in
the country would add game birds. After the meal would come
the sweets and confections, then perhaps some spiced wine or
even whole spices, which were thought to aid in digestion.

Very likely you are congratulating us moderns because we
certainly don't eat and drink like that! So are we "off the hook"
for gluttony? For the most part, only vestiges of *this* kind of glut-

tony remain in our fat-sensitive culture: the "all you can eat for $4.95" buffet, or the 800-pound man who must be taken from his bed by crane through a special opening in the wall when he goes to the hospital. These days, gluttony of the medieval sort stands out like an elephant in a pet store window. *Nevertheless, the sin of gluttony is alive and well.*

And there are more kinds of gluttony than stoking a ravenous appetite. To be sure, the word itself comes from the Latin *gluttire*, which means "to swallow," "to gulp down." But the moral deformity of this vice includes various other unreasonable approaches to alimentation. To quote St. Thomas Aquinas, eating "too soon, too expensively, too much, too eagerly, or with too much finicky fussing about your food" is to practice the sin of gluttony.[4]

The Tool Is Self-Control

For John Cassian, the fourth-century monastic who brought the concept of the Seven Deadly Sins to Europe, the primary goal regarding appetite was training in self-control. This fruit of the Spirit was considered so important that persons desiring admission to a monastic order had to lie outside the monastery for ten days, thereafter undergoing many humiliations and tests of obedience, all to develop self-control. Therefore, learning to battle gluttony was of primary importance; here is what Cassian wrote about gluttony:

> The first conflict we must enter upon is that against gluttony, which we have explained as the pleasures of the palate: and in the first place as we are going to speak of the system of fasts, and the quality of food, we must again recur to the traditions and customs of the Egyptians,[5] as everybody knows that they contain a more advanced discipline in the matter of self-control, and a perfect method of discrimination.[6]

Cassian and others of his time realized that food in too great abundance could intoxicate and that the correct way of dealing with food and drink was the way of modification and even bod-ily chastening. The idea was to learn to exercise "restraint in the matter of the food, which we are obliged to take owing to the necessity of supporting the body. A reasonable supply of food taken daily is better than excessive fasting, which can weaken the power of prayers by weakening the body."

These monks asked a good (rhetorical) question: "How can control over the bodily appetite for food be lacking and yet a man control the more powerful temptations to unchastity?" In other words, if you can't even manage your passion for hot-fudge-drenched ice cream, how do you expect to control the suasion of the much more powerful tugging of the sex drive? Cassian answers: "So therefore the foundation and basis of the spiritual combat must be laid in the struggle against gluttony." That is, begin with the basics; learn the habit of self-control early. Do you have problems controlling the pursuit of pleasure? Cassian is implying that you can learn. Start practicing by con-trolling your less demanding impulses and progress to the more insistent.

Most of us will have some difficulty with these ancient writ-ings on gluttony (and lust, too) because we are not monks. As some, including John Cassian, have opposed lust to celibacy rather than to chastity, so they have opposed gluttony to absti-nence from food, and for similar reasons. The monk's discipline included regular and frequent fasting; violation of that discipline could conveniently and correctly be classified as gluttony. But for people like us whose religious obligations may not include the discipline of regular fasting, gluttony has usually been de-fined in terms of deviation in the direction of excess from some mean.[7]

Total abstinence from solid food might not be the best idea as a first effort for those who haven't practiced fasting at all. The senior pastor of our church recently called us to a forty-day Lenten fast. If that sounds like a mammoth enterprise calling for impossible feats of self-control, you might consider, as I'm sure many in our congregation did, a more moderate program of self-denial. The point here is to develop the skill of self-control with practice.

At just what point concern with the pleasures of taste becomes gluttony has always been difficult to determine in real-life situations. Jesus complained that many of his contemporaries suffered from this difficulty:

> "But to what shall I compare this generation? It is like children sitting in the market places and calling to their playmates, 'We piped to you, and you did not dance; we wailed, and you did not mourn.'
>
> "For John came neither eating nor drinking, and they say, 'He has a demon'; the Son of man came eating and drinking, and they say, 'Behold, a glutton and a drunkard, a friend of tax collectors and sinners.' Yet wisdom is justified by her deeds" (Matthew 11:16–19).

Small deviations are as difficult to discriminate here as they are in any kind of measurement. How do you discern such vague traits as "inordinate and excessive concern with gastronomic pleasures"? What's excessive when it comes to pleasures that are not wrong in themselves? It isn't easy, but it is important. Signs of sin include "demanding too exquisite dishes" and "requiring too great care in preparation of food."[8] Again the little adverb "too" makes the cutting line hard to locate. But what these phrases tell us is that one need not weigh three hundred pounds to be gluttonous. A man may be lithe as Tarzan or a woman tubular as Twiggy, but if a person finds that she is preoccupied with fine flavors, gourmet restaurants, choice wines, or *anything* else to the point where God is obscured, duties are neglected, or the neighbor's need is forgotten, the preoccupation is gluttony. Are you able to judge for yourself when and to what extent you are neglecting the service of God and the love of your neighbor because you are so preoccupied with pleasures of the palate?

Spiritual, Aesthetic, and Other Kinds of Gluttony

In its wider sense, according to Spain's John of the Cross (ca. A.D. 542), gluttony can also be aesthetic, intellectual, or spiritual. Since joy comes only from God, John believed that someone who seeks to draw happiness from the world is like "a famished person who opens his mouth to satisfy himself with air." He taught that only by breaking the rope of our desires could we fly up to God. Above all, he was concerned for those who suffered dryness or depression in their spiritual life, and he offered encouragement that God loved them and was leading them deeper into faith.

"What more do you want, O soul! And what else do you search for outside, when within yourself you possess your riches, delights, satisfaction and kingdom—your beloved whom you desire and seek? Desire him there, adore him there. Do not go in pursuit of him outside yourself. You will only become distracted and you won't find him, or enjoy him more than by seeking him within you."[9]

But while he delighted in the enjoyment of God's presence, John of the Cross believed it could be as dangerous to get hooked on spiritual delights as to become addicted to worldly pleasures—even if these pleasures are encountered in church. Do you go into a tailspin of disappointment when you don't get any special "good feelings" during devotions, any sensory experience of God in prayer or worship? Do you give up praying when you *feel* nothing unique or exciting?

Have you ever thought that even good things—no, *especially* good things—can become objects of gluttony? Arlene's story can help us to understand.

Arlene's Intervention

It was Saturday morning, a time in many houses for relaxation, coffee, and maybe a pancake breakfast. Arlene had not stopped to think how unusual was the request of her family that she stay home for the next few hours. She was active, busy, and often gone from home. As the children grew older, she found more time to do things at church. But today she remained at the house—and a good thing, too. With important work to do, she was entrenched in her home office. The computer keyboard was clicking when the front doorbell chimed. *Oh, well, Roger will take care of it.* He was downstairs, and besides, she had a major project to finish. Another distracting chime from the doorbell. *Mormon missionaries, maybe? Jehovah's Witnesses?* She forced herself back to her task. She simply *had* to finish the brochures, advertisements, and signs for the church rummage sale. And she *had* to do it today.

"Mom?" Jeremy called. "Mom, can you come in here for a little while?" her fourteen-year-old asked.

Now what? "Honey, not at the moment. I'm awfully busy," she yelled, telling herself she would do something nice with the kids later.

"But we need to talk to you. It's very important. Please come in here."

We? She wondered what could be so pressing. Shrugging, she decided to leave the PC on. Whatever this was, it wouldn't take long. Pushing her chair back, she stood up, scribbled a note reminding herself to include a line or two about the refreshments for the sale, and went to find Jeremy. When she entered the living room, she did a double take. There were her sister, Jewel, and her brother, Jack, sitting in her living room with Roger and the kids! Arlene panicked. Had she forgotten something?

"Sweetheart, we need to talk to you," Roger began. "We have something to say to you, and we're going to take turns around the circle. Let's start with Anna."

The ten-year-old had been thinking all morning about what she would say. "Mom, we all got together because we want you to know how important you are to us." Arlene opened her mouth to speak, but Pam continued: "We don't like it that you are up at church so much. We want you to stay home and stop going to so many meetings." Arlene couldn't believe her ears as she heard her oldest daughter run through the days of the past week, naming for each night the church activity her mother had attended each evening.

Jeremy, looking earnest and a little tense, began to speak before she could reply to Anna: "We really missed you a lot on every one of those nights. And we want you to stop working on some of those programs and going to some of those organization meetings and stay home with us. We're all feeling as though we don't even know our mother."

Jack was next. Arlene had always looked to her big brother for wisdom, but now she felt herself getting a bit irritated. "Sis," Jack began, "we've watched you ever since you came to the Lord. At first, your commitment was really personal and spiritual. But somewhere along the line—well, things changed." He couldn't go on, looked at Jewel.

This was difficult for them all, and it was very hard for Jewel, Arlene's younger sister. She had grown up admiring Arlene and still respected her so much that to join in this intervention seemed utterly impossible. Forcing herself to speak, she picked up where Jack left off. "It's like you started getting hooked on a drug—only the 'drug' was church activities. At first you were thrilled with knowing Jesus himself and you led us all to Him, but then you gradually slid over into having to go to anything connected with church. I know most of these things are important, but . . ."

It was Roger's turn. "Love, we all know the programs at church are for the most part important and worthwhile, but you're needed here as well, and too much of the time we're here while you're there. For us, your family, this has become a problem. I don't want to be making a mistake here, so I've talked this over with Pastor Engelder because I didn't want to interfere with other things the Lord calls you to be and do. He agreed that church activities can get in the way of family life, and he suggested that the family—all of us—tell you about how much we need you and ask you to cut out some of the activities you're engaged in and spend several nights a week here with us."

Arlene felt hot tears running down her cheeks, felt herself getting furious. "And how do you know what the Lord wants me to do? How does Pastor Engelder know? I thought he appreciated my contribution! I thought the church wanted my help. This is too much." She wanted to scream. She wanted to run. She hadn't expected this. And especially she hadn't expected her own brother and sister *and* the pastor to push her out of her church activities! She'd never heard of such a thing.

"Mom, we didn't want to make you mad," Jeremy spoke softly and sincerely. "We want you to be glad to know you are too important to us to not speak up to you instead of just complaining to one another like we have been when you're gone so much."

Anna wasn't so reticent. "I don't see why you have to get upset and yell at us, Mom. Why don't you just listen like you tell us to do when someone wants to ask us to change something? Aren't we your family? Don't you want to know when we feel bad about something you're doing?"

"Well, yes," conceded Arlene, feeling a little less like a child being disciplined by her parents and beginning to feel a little more like Roger and the kids might have a point. "Maybe I have been gone a bit too much. But, Roger, it makes me mad that you had to turn this into a court proceeding and that you had to drag Jack and Jewel into it. And the pastor, too! Couldn't you have handled this yourself?"

"No, Arlene," replied Roger. "All of us, the kids and I, have asked you more than once to change things. But it wasn't getting through. It was so much like you were addicted to something. I don't know, I'm not an expert on addiction, but in many ways your actions were the same. Like you refused to take it seriously—you made vague promises to change, and you went right on increasing the 'dose' of church activity. I guess it's easy to confuse church programs with the God they're meant to serve. To become a 'church junkie.' I don't blame you for feeling a little angry about all this, but will you please, when you feel a little less upset, pray about it? Ask the Lord whether He isn't speaking through your family."

Well, Arlene did calm down. Then she found it possible to listen. She had to concede that her family had a strong case. She prayed for God's enlightenment, and as she thought about what He might be saying, came face to face with the fact that she was a "church junkie." She was a glutton. Not a food glutton like Henry VIII, not an alcoholic or a pot smoker, but a church glutton. What had happened? She had begun by serving the Lord. Gradually, she began to enjoy the programs, the activities, the sense of importance, the pleasure of accomplishment, and the interactions with other brothers and sisters in the family of God. And this enjoyment, as long as it was a bonus, was a good. But at some point there was a shift. Arlene found herself hooked on the pleasure. And at that point the deadly sin began. All this insight developed AFTER she listened to the pleas of those who loved her, and she turned to the Lord for counsel on that about which she had never even dreamed she was in need of change.

She made some important alterations. Arlene finally was home regularly all but one or two evenings a week—a very happy family had their recovering church glutton back! Their efforts to speak the truth in love together had borne fruit. Some readers will recognize that what they did is, in addiction-treatment circles, called "an intervention."

Any attachments can become objects of gluttony—of desire that demands such dedication to a pleasure that it virtually overwhelms our soul's desire for God. The pursuit of the pleasures connected with intellectual activity, the arts, literature, music, or even religious experiences may become important enough to preoccupy the gluttonous character. We sometimes speak of our relationship with these things in terms of good or bad *taste,* or of *savoring, devouring, feasting the eyes upon, drinking in, drooling over, finding sustenance in,* and *digesting.* Such figures of speech derived from gastrointestinal imagery suggest that sins of "too much, too soon, too expensive, too eager, and with too much fuss" can be applied as well to overconcern with so-called "higher" pleasures as to food and drink. Even low-brow attachments to such things as TV and spectator sports can become objects of gluttonous consumption.

Boredom—The Pleasure Trap

The gluttonous character, like the lustful person, is precisely Kierkegaard's *aesthete,* the one who lives for pleasure. What Kierkegaard pointed to was the total dedication to better and better pleasure displayed by the accomplished hedonist. The better endowed he is with intellect, knowledge, discrimination, and energy, the more successful he is at achieving pleasure and enjoyment. It is almost certain that many of us will find the personality of the clever and able aesthetic or spiritual glutton more fascinating than characters dominated by pride, envy, anger, greed, or sloth—especially if lust contends with gluttony for first place on his sin profile.

Kierkegaard's special contribution to the discussion of hedonism is his brilliant demonstration of its failure to yield what it promises. Yes, pleasure is out there to be had—at first. But the problem is that no matter how he tries to avoid it, the aesthete-hedonist-glutton at last gets bored with even the most titillating objects and pursuits. And at the end he runs out of material.

Tyler—A Case of Boredom

With my first look at Tyler, calmly reading an old copy of *Health Bulletins* in the waiting room, I was certain his presenting complaint would prove most unusual. Muscular, neatly groomed, probably in his late twenties, dressed in a sweatshirt and baggy trousers, with dark wavy hair and even features, he looked like a young man on very good terms with himself. Like a confident salesman, accustomed to closing the deal he wanted, he looked me straight in the eye when I called his name. What psychological difficulty would trouble a man like this? How could he have a debilitating problem?

I had looked over his test results. Well enough within normal limits, they described a person above normal in intelligence, relaxed, collected, accustomed to doing as he liked, and seldom at the mercy of his impulses. According to his social history he had earned a black belt in karate. He would probably not tell me a story of depression, gnawing guilt, fretfulness, or pointless anxiety. Drugs? Alcohol? Maybe, but I doubted it.

Without waiting for my question, he began: "I'm totally bored." What an opening! I thought I had heard every conceivable presenting issue, but I had never before encountered this one. (Not because boredom is uncommon—Blaise Pascal even observed that, in his opinion, boredom is the natural state of man.[10]) I flashed on a momentary recollection of one of my daughters at sixteen. She had a well-used habit of condemning whatever she found undesirable with a single awful word: "BORING!" (This was pronounced with the first syllable elongated indefinitely: "BO-O-O-OORING!")

As best I could recollect, no client had ever before asked me to treat a case of boredom. Ironically, however, most people never grow out of their dread of boredom. Rather, they do all they can to avoid it, constantly seeking novel circumstances and fresh entertainment. Bored with vocations, spouses, dwellings, toys, and life itself, human nature changes externals and expects thereby to be cured. Theological seminaries have been experiencing an upsurge in what are called "late vocations." Realizing that money and technology have not delivered the contentment they had assumed a good job would bring them, people are hoping a new spiritual career might fill the void.

What, then, did Tyler expect? How should I respond? I hadn't the least idea. So I reverted to a time-honored but productive device, always available to a counselor who hasn't a clue where to go next: "Tell me more about it," I urged. It was a serviceable but not creative response. Yet it turned out to be all he needed to get him going.

"I have everything," he said, with a sour expression on his face as if it were a curse. This was a man who was not content though his dreams were fulfilled. On the contrary, he spelled out the unsatisfactory conditions most people would hardly consider dire straits.

"My wife and I have plenty of money. Incidentally, don't worry about your fee. I'm aware that my insurance won't pay for these sessions, but that's okay. I have a six-figure income and my wife makes more money than I do. Besides, her parents have lots of money, and they can't wait to buy us things. I have stocks and a collection of rare coins valued in the million-dollar range. There'll be no problem with compensation."

"Okay, you're rich—and spending money hasn't cured your

boredom," I replied, a little peeved at myself for my own envious thoughts about how nice it would be to have his problem. I didn't like my resentment that this whiner "had it so good." Why couldn't he quit complaining and appreciate his wealth? Was I put off because he seemed to be bragging? Why was he taking up my time? Because he could pay for it?

You have to listen to me even if I don't have what you consider a serious clinical issue because I can buy and sell you. Is that what I was hearing him say? But whatever his motives might have been, weren't my own sinful envy and greed the roots of my difficulties with him? It occurred to me that God was holding training sessions for him *and for me!* I yanked my thoughts into line with those of my Counselor and silently repented. My irritation forgiven, I realized that this man would never consult a therapist just to buy bragging rights. He was in trouble. And if we were going to continue, I would have to change my own attitude.

He had already sensed my cynicism, and he wasn't intimidated. "I don't think you understand, Doctor. I'm not just passing the time of day. I thought that, as a behavioral expert, you could give me some suggestions for overcoming boredom. I'm sure I haven't tried everything."

"No, of course not. I guess nobody could try *everything*. But aren't there one or two answers you have already tried and found helpful?"

He took a moment to think. "New toys have usually helped me feel better for a little while: snowmobiles, pool tables, boats, fast cars. But I have to work harder all the time to make myself believe in such things. They have become less effective, less engaging, more like a rich dessert stuffed into an engorged stomach. I can have anything I want, pretty much. But I'm really hurting. I'm sure this isn't what you usually hear from a client, but I need something. Please take this seriously: I'm bored. I don't know what to do about it."

Now, ashamed of myself, I apologized to God for my failure to attend to the only thing that mattered to my patient: his own wretchedness. Then I looked into my own memory banks for truth. As Pascal expressed it, "Man finds nothing so intolerable as to be in a state of complete rest, without passions, without occupation, without diversion, without effort. Then he faces his nullity, loneliness, inadequacy, dependence, helplessness, emptiness. And at once there wells up from the depths of his soul boredom, gloom, depression, chagrin, resentment, despair."[11] That was Tyler! The cool front was a cover over his own tooth-and-nail battle against relentlessly advancing despair.

I had to level with him. "I must admit to you that I am perplexed. It isn't that I think you aren't perfectly well entitled to consult a psychologist. It's simply that at this point I haven't the slightest idea how to help you. If you like, we can meet again. Maybe you will be able to tell me more."

Though our session was over, he had already planned to schedule another appointment. I can't imagine why, in view of my abysmal failure to even pretend that I could assist in curing his boredom! On top of that, my countertransference feelings were anything but righteous! (Countertransference is simply the counselor's emotional reaction to the client.) Maybe he appreciated my honesty; more likely, he didn't know where else to turn. At least his promise to return gave me time to think about the problem.

At our next session, Tyler was a little less upbeat but curious about what, if anything, I might suggest. I think his expectations this time were somewhat lower, which made me more comfortable with my own helplessness. He seemed a little sad: "It has been a little disappointing for me that you didn't have any idea what to do about boredom. I was hoping you could help."

"I don't blame you for being disappointed. What have you tried to do about this problem yourself?"

"Everything. I've tried everything I can think of. You know I've changed careers several times. This helps for a while, but I get bored again—and lately the relapse has been occurring sooner. One thing I have always used is distraction, like finding some entertainment or playing with new gadgets. I buy things for fun, things like my new truck, or a classy boat, a snow-mobile, a home theater—you name it. The Internet was fun until I got tired of it. As I said, some of this helps at first. But before too long, I'm bored with the toys I have—just the way I was as a kid. My mom complained about me being hard to keep entertained. She would sometimes go to the store and get a new toy for me just to keep me out of her hair for a while. I've tried hobbies, entertainment, working out for hours at the club, even discussion groups. And they all work for a time—but never for long. You know, sometimes I've even wished we were poor. I actually envy the guy next door who has to get up every morning and work all day just to keep his rent paid."

I was still failing miserably to catch on to the simple truth! So I tried a pretty lame offer: "I could give you a vocational interest test. Maybe we could find a calling you'd really like."

"I've already taken three of them. And not one came back with a clear recommendation. The counselors said my interests are too scattered over too many areas to make the tests work well. You need a focus, apparently, for the tests to make strongly successful predictions. Man, if I had a focus I wouldn't need the test!"

A light went on inside my brain. I suddenly saw what was wrong with Tyler, and I knew I wouldn't find it in the diagnostic manual for psychologists. *This was a spiritual disorder.* And it was now so obvious I would have seen it sooner if I hadn't been looking for a psychological problem and a scientific solution. I could see that we had to take a different direction.

"What is your first principle?" I asked, blurting out the question, realizing before I finished that I would need to explain. He wouldn't be likely to know what I meant.

He didn't! "Huh? I don't get it. What are you talking about?" At least his adrenaline had started flowing.

"Let me explain. Everybody, whether they know it or not, lives for something; something so important to them that it motivates everything they choose, everything they do. It's the reason they are willing to get out of bed in the morning; something of such importance that, if necessary, they would die for it. Some philosophers have called it a 'first principle.' For some people the aim of life is money, for some it's family, for some it's health, or truth, or beauty, or whatever. What is yours?"

"Gosh, I never thought about that. What is my 'thing'—my first principle—what do I live for?" He closed his eyes and said nothing for a while. I let him think it over. He seemed to be lost in a sort of mental maze. Then he answered, "I don't get it. I just know I'm not finding happiness, whatever the cause is. That's why I'm here. And I haven't the faintest idea where this conversation is going. How do I know what I'm living for? I never considered it. I've just tried to get whatever I thought would keep me feeling positive, upbeat, interested in life. I just want to be happy, I guess. I'm aiming for—excitement, pleasure, feeling good, getting rid of this bored feeling. Aren't we supposed to be happy?"

"Maybe you've just come up with the answer," I replied. "How about this? Your first principle is pursuing pleasure and excitement, feeling happy. You might try reviewing your life and asking yourself if that aptly describes what you have been living for, the aim of life and of all you do."

"Yeah, I see where you're going. You're asking me to look at my life, at what I *do* and *don't do*, rather than at what I say. Something tells me you're on the right track. I *do* all kinds of things, some good, some bad, some stupid, some sensible. But it's true—in all my choices I'm thinking of what will spare me unpleasant feelings like boredom and what will give me pleasant feelings like excitement. I guess that is my first principle, as you labeled it."

"Now let's call it something else, Tyler. Another way to ask the question of first principles is this: What is the name of the god you really serve? Because whatever you are actually living for *is* your god, regardless of what you say about the matter, and regardless of what you think you *should* be living for. Jesus once described it as seeking something first, as going after something so important you'd give anything to get it. And He said that if you choose to seek the right thing, you'll not only obtain it, you'll get all the other good things you're no longer putting in first place—like a bonus."

"Yeah, I suppose that's possible," he responded thoughtfully.

"But how do I know for sure what I live for? It's all so abstract and wordy. How do I *know*? I'm supposed to be living for God, right? How can I tell if my heart is really set on Him? I go to church most Sundays. But it's not much help. My church is pretty boring, too."

"Things are boring because what you're looking for is excitement and pleasure. You're looking for real life in things outside of real life. This dedication to gorging on excitement and pleasure is one manifestation of the sinful trait of gluttony. Another name for this kind of gluttony is hedonism. When pleasure rather than God's kingdom becomes life's biggest concern, your first principle is that you're a hedonist, a glutton for good feelings. In your case, the sin of gluttony is the pursuit of happiness as your ultimate concern. If your overriding purpose in life is to spare yourself pain and keep yourself in a state of pleasant feelings, you will probably have a measure of success for a while. But—and this is the reason hedonism doesn't work—nothing will keep you in a state of high good feelings forever. Everything you hitch your life to will function exactly like alcohol, overeating, or drugs. You will need more and different things, more change, new ideas and fresh experiences, and eventually, as with drugs, the novelty wears off and stops working so it's harder to find the new thing with which to turn yourself on. When this doesn't work any more, we call the resulting misery boredom. And that's what you are suffering from. When did you decide to live for pleasure?"

I was sure he had never consciously and deliberately chosen pleasure as his god. Most of us don't intentionally decide to live our lives for nice feelings. Sinful humankind, unaltered by the Spirit of God, just naturally lives to get good feelings and avoid bad ones and thinks this is obviously and self-evidently the purpose of existing. But God never made us simply to pursue pleasant emotions. Boredom is God's device for sounding an alarm, trying to make us aware that, "You are serving the wrong god." If people ignore the alarm, distracting themselves with things, changing circumstances more and more rapidly, they just naturally live and die as hedonists, gluttons for pleasure.

Tyler's reply confirmed my expectations: "I can't remember ever actually resolving, 'I am going to base my life on getting the most pleasure and happiness I can find and keeping myself too busy to think of the bad stuff.' It just came naturally, I think."

The room got quiet—very quiet—as both of us came face to face with the total worthlessness of the universal human delusion, the belief that gluttonous pleasure-seeking is magic. We both saw how, without some kind of major change, the majority of human beings will continue to live without giving any thought to their gluttony. *Hedonism is a natural state of sinful humankind.*

Tyler was now both more miserable and more hopeful than when he had begun. "You know, I don't think I've ever made a decision about what's vital and important to me, about what to live for. I've just assumed that the point of life is to keep feeling as good as I can and keep avoiding the bad experiences, even avoiding thinking about them."

I was pleased at how Tyler was now thinking, and I didn't want to raise distracting roadblocks, so I just nodded and said, "Uh huh," another time-honored counseling mechanism.

He continued. "I guess I could decide to live for something else. I could decide to dedicate my life to something important, something that really matters. Like helping others, or taking care of my family, or . . . or . . . even serving God."

"Did you ever think about consulting Jesus' wisdom on this subject? He said in several different ways that if you aim at serving God's will, or determine to pursue God's kingdom, even to the point of laying your whole life at His feet and trying your best to obey His teachings in all you do, that you would find the most valuable thing there is, God and His kingdom, and that as an additional gift, you would also enjoy the good things (like pleasure) you aren't even trying for."

"You mean it's kind of paradoxical? If I aim at possessions, money, good feelings, fun, I won't find anything in life that is truly worthwhile—maybe He meant I'd end up bored. But if I aim at something else, higher, better, more along the lines of serving and pleasing God, obeying Jesus' teachings, really meaning it when I say He is my Lord, then I'd get a different result—the very happiness and fulfillment I'm NOT aiming for. Is that it?"

Tyler did find a cure for boredom. He started reading the New Testament and got interested in what Jesus has to say about how to live. He found the power of scriptural teaching taking hold of his life until he wanted to dedicate himself completely to the Lord who died for him on the cross so he might receive God as King in his life. He decided to cooperate with the Holy Spirit, learning to use his will to make decisions based on obedience to the will of God rather than on what might feel good. And his boredom—he had to battle it by a clear process of checking himself out, asking himself what he was trying to do now, whether it was to make himself happy or to please and serve God. Immediately he discovered he had been seeking "all these things" instead of the kingdom, and he would endeavor to change his behavior. And change his behavior it did. I can't go into detail here, but Tyler became a man whose time filled up with deeds of love toward God and others. He didn't spend much time asking himself if he was still bored, but if you had put the question to him he would probably have been puzzled. Boredom was the furthest thing from his mind. Nor was he continually asking himself if he was happy. He rather occupied himself with the question, "Lord, what do You want me to do now?" The cure Tyler experienced was the therapy of God's kingdom, the pearl of great price, the treasure hidden in the field.

Is Boredom Our Greatest Fear These Days?

Why is hedonism such a threat, especially in our time? Both the great mathematician Pascal and the philosopher Kierkegaard agree that for modern man, the evil by which he feels most threatened is boredom. Kierkegaard depicts the hedonist as complaining that "boredom is the root of all evil. What wonder, then, that the world goes from bad to worse . . . as boredom increases."[12]

According to this thinker, modern man—the hedonist—sees nothing to life except feelings. Pleasures and pains, interests and boredoms. Rarely do we notice how commonly we eat and drink, read and converse, turn the equipment on and off, surf the Internet without a particular aim, and leave our houses to "go somewhere," simply because we are gluttons for pleasure and interest. The point to be remembered is that even if the glutton succeeds in avoiding coarse habits, dangerous obesity, and frequent drunken stupors, the concerns to which he devotes his life are ultimately going to betray him—not because he finds pleasures good, but because he makes pleasures his ultimate, his God. And they aren't capable of performing in that place. So the glutton refuses to let God be God. The result is his own undoing.

A Memorable Tale from Aesop

A number of flies were attracted to a jar of honey that had been overturned in a housekeeper's room. Placing their feet in it, they ate greedily. Their feet, however, became so smeared with the honey that they could not use their wings, nor release themselves, and they were suffocated. Just as they were expiring, they exclaimed, "O foolish creatures that we are, for the sake of a little pleasure we have destroyed ourselves."

Whether we get our feet stuck in music, books, paintings, TV, football, golf, or *anything* else, we learn that our gluttony can destroy us.

Scripture on Gluttony

Perhaps the most chilling Bible passage condemning gluttony occurs among the theocratic political laws in the book of Deuteronomy. As I understand it, this is a part of the criminal law for the nation of Israel, and it was not meant to be taken as a universal moral requirement:

> If a man have a stubborn and rebellious son, which will not obey the voice of his father, or the voice of his mother, and that, when they have chastened him, will not hearken

unto them: Then shall his father and his mother lay hold on him, and bring him out unto the elders of his city, and unto the gate of his place; And they shall say unto the elders of his city, This our son is stubborn and rebellious, he will not obey our voice; he is a glutton, and a drunkard. And all the men of his city shall stone him with stones, that he die: so shalt thou put evil away from among you; and all Israel shall hear, and fear (Deuteronomy 21:18–21 KJV).

Although this prescription was not a part of God's moral law, its sobering message is clear: Gluttony and rebellious focus on pleasure cannot be tolerated.

John Cassian cites St. Paul on the subject of self-control:

"I," said he, "so run, not as uncertainly; I so fight, not as one that beateth the air: but I chastise my body and bring it into subjection, lest by any means when I have preached to others I myself should be a castaway." You see how he made the chief part of the struggle depend upon himself, that is upon his flesh, as if on a most sure foundation, and placed the result of the battle simply in the chastisement of the flesh and the subjection of his body. He does not run uncertainly, because, looking to the heavenly Jerusalem, he has a mark set, towards which his heart is swiftly directed without swerving. He does not run uncertainly, because, "forgetting those things which are behind, he reaches forth to those that are before, pressing towards the mark for the prize of the high calling of God in Christ Jesus," whither he ever directs his mental gaze. . . .

Proverbs 23:20–21 (KJV) says, "Be not among winebibbers; among riotous eaters of flesh: For the drunkard and the glutton shall come to poverty: and drowsiness shall clothe a man with rags."

Gluttony in the Sin Test

You may wonder whether in the Sin Test experimental items were included that would tap into spiritual, aesthetic, and intellectual gluttony, and if so, whether these traits were shown to be correlated with traditional food/drink gluttony. The answer is *yes* to both. Here are some items that did seem to be measuring a general trait: gluttony, which would include physical, aesthetic, and spiritual forms of gluttony. Record your True or False responses in the spaces provided.

F 1. I am one of those people who gets so totally engrossed in the appreciation of religious art that I forget the religious significance temporarily.

F 2. I get so much pleasure out of the feeling of God's nearness and fellowship that I find myself concentrating on the enjoyment rather than on God and His will.

F 3. I think it would be ideal to be in a constant state of ecstasy.

These items on spiritual and aesthetic gluttony were significantly correlated with items like the following about *gustatory* gluttony.

F 4. Frequently I find that I have eaten so much I just don't feel like doing anything but lying around.

T 5. I often think of eating between meals.

F 6. One of the things I would like most to do if I had plenty of money is keep a well-stocked liquor collection.

T 7. It is easy for me to enjoy rich and tasty desserts even after I know I have eaten enough and feel full.

F 8. Much of the time I have to be concerned about my weight since I tend to be heavier than I should be.

F 9. Others have told me seriously that I should eat less between meals.

F 10. I spend more money on alcoholic beverages than I give to God.

For Further Thought and Discussion

1. What do you think of the ancient identifying marks of gluttonous consumption behavior: "too much, too soon, too ex-

pensive, too eager, and with too much fuss"? Would these help you to identify gluttony in yourself? Would they be applicable to hedonistic and spiritual gluttony as well as to food/drink gluttony?

2. What do you think about St. Paul's way of dealing with gluttony and gaining self-control (1 Corinthians 9:27) by "pommelling" his body? What might this phrase mean? How could you apply it to the various kinds of gluttony?

3. Do you practice fasting? Has it helped you to control your appetites generally? Would the practice of fasting help you to develop self-control?

4. How is most contemporary gluttony different from Henry VIII's gluttony?

5. St. John of the Cross introduced the idea of three kinds of gluttony. What are they? Do you think his concepts are applicable to people today?

6. Do you think Clement's instructions for appropriate behav-

ior at the table are still applicable today? Would you add anything else? Change anything?

7. Why was Jesus labeled a glutton by some of his contemporaries?

You will remember that you earlier saw the form below. Before you turned to the chapters on the Seven Deadly Sins themselves, you encountered a form for ranking the sins according to their degree of influence on your own behavior. It may be that studying the sins has worked a change in your rankings. Without first looking back to consult the way you ordered the sins before, rank them again, according to your present perception of yourself. Then you can consult the form you completed at the end of chapter 1. Compare the two forms. What, if anything, has changed?

Individually Rank-Ordering the Seven Deadly Sin Traits

You can use this sheet for rank-ordering yourself or someone else on the Seven Cardinal Sins. The trait on which you consider yourself to score highest is #1. The one on which you are lowest is #7. If you are ranking a friend or a spouse, use the same system. Feel free to make copies of this form if you wish to share it with someone else.

___2___ PRIDE: Being desirous of occupying first place; seeking to have authority over others; detesting being under authority or external restraints; overestimating self or one's own abilities and gifts; exhibiting blindness to good qualities in others; showing contempt for others; being anxious to get credit; having presumptuous ambition; taking on tasks without the ability to perform them; thriving on praise and recognition; boasting or faking self-deprecation; being shocked with the misdeeds and faults of others; being self-satisfied; being thrilled or enamored with one's own spiritual and moral achievements; being strongly opinionated, inflexible, or argumentative; chafing under the rule and sovereignty of God.

_1_ ENVY: Habitually being in competition with others; feeling unhappy when another gets a break; being glad when others (especially those perceived as "equals") have setbacks or troubles; losing "self-esteem" when another is perceived as having more (spirituality, attractiveness, popularity, intelligence, material rewards—anything) than oneself; desiring to expose defects in others; frequently interpreting others' words and deeds as bad; persistently tuning in to compare self with others—their qualities, possessions, achievements, etc.

_3_ ANGER: Having a strong desire for revenge; cultivating and harboring resentment; thinking about getting even; arguing, quarreling, fighting; being primarily silent and sullen; being sarcastic, cynical, insulting, critical; frequently being indignant; desiring harm for others; considering it right to "settle the score."

_6_ GREED: Wanting to accumulate material things just for the sake of possessing them; cheating, lying, or stealing to gain or hang on to things; being tightfisted and retentive; being excessively thrifty; being overcautious about spending; hating to give; being stingy; being callous toward the needy; hating to pay debts, avoiding repayment whenever possible; feeling excessive distress at small losses; finding it hard to trust God to provide for needs.

_7_ SLOTH: Being sorrowful in spirit and mind; finding it difficult to have hope; believing effort and work are too

difficult; procrastinating, putting off attending to important matters; deciding prayer or worship is too hard;
being sluggish and heavy; having a will that is weak; feeling it is useless to try to break bad habits; often investing
self in trivial activities; constantly seeking bodily ease and
comfort; preferring idleness to activity; being sad and
spiritually worn out; drifting along in mediocrity; being
dissatisfied and angry with God for not giving feelings of
peace, consolation, and happiness.

 LUST: Being regularly preoccupied with sexual pleasure,
thoughts, and fantasies; thinking about sexual pleasure to
the exclusion of other things; looking at, touching, embracing, or engaging in intercourse with illicit or forbidden sexual objects or activities; persisting in excessive
interest, conversations, or jokes abut sex.

GLUTTONY: Overindulging in pursuit of worldly pleasure; eating too much; eating too fast; being preoccupied
with food; drinking alcohol too often or too much; being
finicky or choosy about food or drink; overly investing in
the enjoyment of gourmet foods, wines, literature, music,
the arts; embracing pursuits that do not meet fulfillment
in God.

Notes

1. Søren Kierkegaard, *Either/Or: A Fragment of Life*, vols. 1 and 2,
   trans. David F. Swenson and Lillian Marvin Swenson (Princeton, N.J.: Princeton University Press, 1949).
2. Clement of Alexandria (c. A.D. 200), a native of Athens, was
   converted to Christianity by Pantaenus, founder of the Cate-
   chetical School at Alexandria (then the intellectual capital of
   the Mediterranean world). Clement eventually succeeded his
   teacher as head of the school, and for over twenty years he la-
   bored effectively as an apologist for the faith and the catechist
   of the faithful. He regarded the science and philosophy of the
   Greeks as being, like the Torah of the Hebrews, a preparation
   for the gospel, and the curriculum of his school undertook to

give his students both a knowledge of the gospel of Christ and a sound education. His speculative theology, his scholarly defense of the faith, and his willingness to meet non-Christian scholars on their own grounds helped to establish the good reputation of Christianity in the world of learning and to prepare the way for his pupil, Origen, the most eminent theologian of Greek Christianity. Clement is not on the present Roman calendar of saints, but he is on the Eastern calendar and many modern revisions of the Anglican calendar (James Kiefer, *The Lectionary*, http://www.satucket.com/lectionary/index.com).

3. From Christian Classics Ethereal Library at Calvin College, Clement of Alexandria, *The Instructor*, book II. http://www.ccel.org/fathers2/ANF–02/anf02–53htm.

4. Cited in Adolphe Tanquery, *The Spiritual Life: A Treatise on Ascetical and Mystical Theology*, trans. Herman Branderis (Tournai, Belgium: Society of St. John the Evangelist Press, 1930), 44.

5. Monks who lived in the Egyptian desert.

6. John Cassian, *The Twelve Books of John Cassian on the Institutes of the Coenobia and the Remedies for the Eight Principal Faults*, book V, chapter I. Internet http://www.osb.org/lectio/cassian/inst/index.html.

7. Anonymous tract, *The Seven Capital Sins*, 1959, 36–39.

8. Thomas J. Slater, *A Manual of Moral Theology* (London: Burns, Oates, & Washburn, Ltd., 1928), 103–104.

9. John of the Cross, "The Dark Night of the Soul," cited in *The Catholic Encyclopedia*, article on Gluttony by Joseph P. DeLaney. http://www.newadvent.org/cathen/.

10. *Mind on Fire: A Faith for the Skeptical and Indifferent*, ed. James M. Houston (Minneapolis: Bethany House Publishers, 1997).

11. Ibid., 73.

12. *A Kierkegaard Anthology*, ed. Robert Bretall (Princeton, N.J.: Princeton University Press, 1951), 22.

Appendix 1

Taking and Scoring the Sin Test

Taking the Sin Test requires complete honesty about your attitudes and behavior. Do not make a special effort to "look good" or to "look bad." Make every effort to be frank and open about yourself. No one needs to see your responses except you and your God. Pray that God will give you a forthright and vulnerable heart as you respond to the items.

You may administer the Sin Test to yourself. After you have answered *all* 280 items, carefully follow the directions for scoring. Use the scoring keys to mark each item you answered in the "sinful" direction. You will need to transform your raw scores (raw scores are the number of items answered in the "sinful" direction) into scaled scores. Scaled scores on all seven scales make it possible to contrast each of your Seven Deadly Sin scores with the others.

Circle True (T) or False (F) for each item. Do not omit any items. If you aren't sure of your answer, choose the response you think most likely to be correct.

Pride Items (Scale 1)

T   F   1. I have rarely had the thought that God plays around with people like puppets.

T   F   2. There just is no respect these days for people who really know what's going on.

T.   F   3. I would like to be a politician with considerable power to get things done.

T   F   4. I don't have many opinions which I hold so strongly that they cannot be changed.

T   F   5. A great many people have wrong ideas about religion simply because they are so limited and incapable of seeing things the way I do.

T   F   6. I often excuse my own mistakes as just due to "bad breaks," but when others make mistakes I tend to conclude that they just don't have what it takes to do things right.

T   F   7. I am usually surprised when someone goes out of his way to please me or to help me.

T   F   8. It makes me quite resentful when others persistently refuse to accept my good ideas and beliefs.

T   F   9. The abilities and good qualities of other people I know frequently impress me so much that I tell others about them.

T   F   10. When I have to talk about myself I try to talk about my shortcomings and my faults.

T   F   11. It doesn't bother me particularly when I learn that someone unimportant to me has a bad opinion of me.

T   F   12. I think that, if given the opportunity, I could solve a great many of the world's difficulties.

T   F   13. What I do and think are none of God's business.

T   F   14. It's too bad so many people without good taste or intelligence have money and position.

T   F   15. I would never insist that what I consider good taste in music, conduct, etc., must be accepted by those around me.

T   F   16. It's better for me to stay out of tempting situations because I know I can easily be led to do wrong.

T   F   17. I can't understand how some people can apologize so
            easily when they have hurt or offended someone.

T   F   18. I can forgive God most things except the innocent
            suffering He allows in the world.

T   F   19. In view of the senseless trouble the world is always in,
            there is little reason to believe that a God exists who
            rules over the universe.

T   F   20. I feel hurt when I discover that I was invited to a party
            to fill in for someone else who could not come.

T   F   21. I can't understand what keeps some people participat-
            ing in groups when they never get the chance to be
            leaders.

T   F   22. People who habitually keep me waiting are demon-
            strating their feeling that I am unimportant.

T   F   23. Things being the way they are, it is best to take care
            of yourself first and then worry about others if you
            have time.

T   F   24. I am morally no better than most other people.

T   F   25. I strongly disagree with those who believe God is an
            invention to support and encourage weak-minded
            people.

T   F   26. I don't mind spending money to make a good impres-
            sion on others.

T   F   27. I have usually found that nearly everyone I have talked
            to for a long time has something to say that interests
            me.

T   F   28. It is easy for me to forgive another person who has
            wronged me.

T   F   29. It is easier for me to talk about current events or sim-
            ilar topics than to talk about my accomplishments or
            achievements.

T   F   30. When I get into a conversation I am uncomfortable
            unless I get people to talk about subjects I know a
            great deal about.

T   F   31. It is not for me, a creature, to criticize the way God
            uses His power to run the universe.

T   F   32. I don't mind being asked to do a humbling job which
            no one else will take.

T   F   33. It is good for me to associate with others who have good qualities which I lack.

T   F   34. I am amused by other people's primitive ideas about God and how He operates.

T   F   35. If other people fail to recognize how good I am, it is because of their limitations.

T   F   36. People who do not seek their own self-interests before they look after the needs of others probably have inferiority feelings.

T   F   37. I feel resentful when others fail to notice and praise me for my achievements.

T   F   38. It seems as though I am often tackling jobs which turn out to be beyond my ability.

T   F   39. One thing I hardly ever do is belittle other people.

T   F   40. Most of my good qualities developed as a result of my own efforts.

T   F   41. I usually feel irritated when I have to take orders from others.

T   F   42. It is too bad the world has so many dull-witted, uninteresting people in it.

T   F   43. People who readily accept advice from others are probably weak and indecisive themselves.

T   F   44. Through long practice I have learned to smile at the frailties of those around me rather than become irritated by them.

T   F   45. I don't resent being interrupted by someone less important than I am.

My raw score for Pride: _____

(Remember: This raw score is to be determined after you have completed the entire Sin Test. Use the scoring key on page 238 to mark each item that is *opposite* the key, indicating you answered in the "sinful" direction.)

Envy Items (Scale 2)

T F 46. Most movie stars are talented, work hard, and deserve the fame they achieve.

T F 47. Even though I know it's not right, I just can't help feeling a little enjoyment when someone at the top of the heap takes a tumble.

T F 48. It doesn't particularly distress me when one of my friends surpasses me in a field where I have worked hard to become competent.

T F 49. I can't recall deliberately failing to give help to someone who is better than I am, when it didn't require a great deal of effort to do so.

T F 50. It doesn't make me sad or jealous to hear one of my associates highly praised.

T F 51. It would give me pleasure to be at a party where someone more popular than I am suffered extreme embarrassment.

T F 52. I take as much pleasure from a friend's success as I would if it were my own.

T F 53. I wish I could get rid of the feelings of inferiority and resentment which the good fortunes of others frequently arouse in me.

T F 54. Anybody would die on the cross if he knew he was God's Son and had an absolute guarantee that he would rise from the dead in three days and go to heaven.

T F 55. When others tell me about the fun they're having, I frequently have a tendency to feel sad.

T F 56. If I heard an associate who was consistently getting more credit than I faulted for a drastic mistake, it would make me feel better.

T F 57. It doesn't disturb me in the slightest to associate with people who are more attractive than I am.

T F 58. I must admit that I enjoy conversations in which the faults and misdeeds of others are being discussed.

T   F   59. People who are famous because of their achievements in sports, literature, art, music, or other fields shouldn't have so much reward and recognition because they got to the top through a combination of good heredity and good luck.

T   F   60. If one of my associates is especially successful at something, I prefer not to hear about it.

T   F   61. I wouldn't experience the slightest pleasure if I heard that a friend who has more money than I suffered a heavy financial loss.

T   F   62. Very virtuous people irritate me.

T   F   63. I like to be around people who are less gifted than I am.

T   F   64. I almost never feel blue or depressed when a friend wins a game and I lose.

T   F   65. I enjoy hearing others talk about their misfortunes.

T   F   66. I don't see why people think the saints are so great since God gave them the breaks most of us just don't get.

T   F   67. I try hard not to rub it in when I discover that I am more fortunate than others in some way.

T   F   68. It certainly gives me no satisfaction to see someone who has been getting all the breaks suffer a setback.

T   F   69. Sometimes when others speak too highly of a mutual acquaintance, I try to point out his/her defects.

T   F   70. It is certainly fair that people who are more wealthy than I am are made to pay a higher proportion of their income in taxes.

T   F   71. I can't help constantly making comparisons between my possessions, spouse, friends, family, etc., and those of other people.

T   F   72. When somebody is promoted over me, I usually give them credit for superior achievement instead of chalking it up to their "pull" with the boss.

T   F   73. The Bible quotation, "To him who has much, more will be given," disturbs me because it strikes me as unfair.

T   F   74. I wouldn't work very hard just to surpass someone else.

T   F   75. I can't help feeling sad or bitter when I hear of one of my school buddies doing much better than I in life.

T   F   76. My response when someone else is shown favoritism by superiors is to be very happy for them rather than to resent them.

T   F   77. One thing that really gets under my skin is the way many people fawn over wealthy families; they shouldn't have any better treatment than I get.

T   F   78. One thing that strikes me as unfair is that God has everything and everybody is supposed to love Him, while I knock myself out and hardly anybody loves me.

T   F   79. People who get all the breaks need to experience a few more troubles.

My raw score for Envy: _____
(Again, this raw score is to be determined after you have completed the entire Sin Test.)

Anger Items (Scale 3)

T   F   80. I am not one of those people who go about ready for a fight.

T   F   81. I really enjoy watching a vicious and bloody boxing match.

T   F   82. When I read about some of the terrible things other people are doing, I am often left with a feeling of outrage and indignation.

T   F   83. I cannot accept the philosophy expressed in the maxim: "An eye for an eye and a tooth for a tooth."

T   F   84. A very poor way to deal with violent people is to beat them down and keep them in order by force.

T   F   85. It would not make me especially happy to be able to think up very clever insults toward others when I need to put them in their place.

T   F   86. I really enjoy a good hot argument.

T   F   87. I seldom get angry at other drivers, even when they cut in front of me illegally.

T   F   88. I hardly ever go around sullen and silent in order to let someone else know he has done something to hurt me.

T   F   89. Sometimes I hit people who have done something to deserve it.

T   F   90. I am justifiably outraged when I think of all the stupidities and cruelties in the world.

T   F   91. I can't stay angry at anyone for very long.

T   F   92. People born in America with all its resources who did not end up rich were probably just wasteful or lazy.

T   F   93. If there is anything I hate, it's having to talk to someone who has done something against my best interests.

T   F   94. I don't care much for books or movies depicting a great deal of fighting or bloodshed.

T   F   95. I secretly feel good when I learn that someone I dislike has gotten into trouble.

T   F   96. Too many people in this world get away with wrongdoing.

T   F   97. I would like to see capital punishment abolished.

T   F   98. I wish I could invent a device which would help the police bring to justice more criminals who now never get caught.

T   F   99. One thing about our society that is not very civilized is that it permits people to beat each other up in the boxing ring.

T   F   100. Sometimes I get so incensed at what other people do that I just can't control myself.

T   F   101. I would not particularly enjoy seeing someone who has insulted me get arrested for a traffic violation.

T   F   102. I can't think of anyone I really hate.

T   F   103. Most religious people are pompous hypocrites, and I would like to tell them so.

T   F   104. When someone behaves in an insulting way toward me, I figure their behavior is their problem so it hardly occurs to me to try to get even.

T   F   105. I have resentments which I have stored up and harbored for years.

T   F   106. There must be something wrong with people who work to prevent cruelty to animals.

T   F   107. When someone deliberately insults or hurts me I think for hours about things I should have said or done to get even.

T   F   108. When I think how many stupid people are allowed to drive on our highways, I get angry.

T   F   109. Frequently I feel frustrated because I cannot think of a way to get even with someone who deserves it.

T   F   110. I know it's wrong, but I sometimes deliberately prolong a fight.

T   F   111. Hardly anybody in this world is so bad he deserves to be killed.

T   F   112. There is nothing like the moment when the villain gets badly beaten in a wrestling match.

T   F   113. When I have to listen to some preacher telling me what God expects me to do and not to do, I get furious.

My raw score for Anger: _____

Greed Items (Scale 4)

T   F   114. One of my major goals in life is to accumulate enough money so I can be sure of a secure future.

T   F   115. Quite often I notice myself thinking of my financial resources accumulating and increasing, while at the same time I notice my concern about God decreasing.

T   F   116. It makes more sense to me to try to "store up treasure in heaven" even if this requires sacrifice on earth than to amass material possessions now.

T   F   117. When I see a magnificent painting or statue of Christ I can't help wanting to own it first and then thinking of the religious significance second or not at all.

T   F   118. I would rather be holy and poor than rich and sinful.

T   F   119. The root of all evil is the love of money.

T   F   120. I must confess that I am probably not as careful and thoughtful about handling my money as I should be.

T   F   121. It was easy for the poor to follow Christ since they didn't have anything to lose anyway.

T   F   122. Quite often I do things like buy winter coats or Christmas toys during the summer because of the satisfaction of getting them at half price.

T   F   123. Taking on the support of a family and acquiring a car and a house wouldn't interfere with or lessen my devotion to God.

T   F   124. One of my major goals in life is to accumulate enough money so I can be sure of a secure future.

T   F   125. I would rather have a life rich in the knowledge and fellowship of God than a basement full of gold.

T   F   126. I usually avoid buying things on credit because I so dislike making payments later.

T   F   127. I don't see why God demands sacrificial giving of me when I have so little and God has everything.

T   F   128. If God really can do everything, I think He should improve the lot of the poor and helpless instead of leaving it up to the rest of us to take care of them.

T   F   129. I would especially enjoy collecting and owning fine and expensive things (for example, furniture, books, jewelry, art objects).

T   F   130. I know from experience that it is more blessed to give than to receive.

T   F   131. I would prefer a high-paying job in which I was less interested to a lower-paying job which interested me very much.

T   F   132. There is a definite personal pleasure and comfort in knowing you have a plump bank account.

T   F   133. If the credit department of a store to which I owe money should forget to bill me, I would simply figure that it's their problem.

T   F   134. It may seem ridiculous, but I save all sorts of insignificant things such as string, rubber bands, paper clips, old magazines, etc., because I so dislike throwing things away.

T   F   135. Better to have plenty of good food on the table than to have money in the bank.

T   F   136. The best thing to do with money is to save it if possible.

T   F   137. When I lose money I get so uncomfortable I can hardly think about anything else.

T   F   138. People who devote their lives to helping others rather than to making money are usually weak, "bleeding-heart" types.

T   F   139. If I had one wish, I would choose to be the richest person in the world.

T   F   140. I get a lot of satisfaction out of giving to a church, charity, or friends in need.

T   F   141. I seldom go out of my way to buy something at a bargain price.

T   F   142. Money is behind all the power in the world, including that of the church.

T   F   143. I simply can't understand people who through careless spending have financial difficulties.

T   F   144. In matters of material security it is certainly important to remember that "God helps those who help themselves."

T   F   145. My eternal soul is so precious to me that no amount of money could bring me to sell out to the devil.

T   F   146. God may be all-powerful, but you can usually accomplish a lot more through money than through prayers.

T   F   147. Poor people should work harder to help themselves instead of so often relying on the rest of us for help.

T   F   148. It doesn't bother me very much to buy something rather expensive and then discover later that I could have gotten it for less at another store.

T   F   149. If I knew I could get away with it, I would do something I know to be wrong to acquire a substantial sum of money.

T   F   150. I would like to own the Vatican with all its cultural treasures and just roam around through it and charge admission to visitors.

T   F   151. When entertaining I would rather have food and re-freshments left over than provide just enough and thus avoid waste.

T   F   152. It is easier to forget that someone else owes me a little money than that I owe someone else.

T   F   153. If I received a gift of $100 I would rather spend it for some enjoyable recreation than put it in the bank.

T   F   154. I couldn't care less what people think of me as long as I have plenty of money.

T   F   155. I would rather have a job at which I could relax and make less money than a job which paid a great deal and demanded a lot of effort.

T   F   156. The worry and responsibility connected with possess-ing great wealth makes riches more trouble than they are worth.

T   F   157. A priest talks to God but listens to money, since he is as worried as anyone about his livelihood.

T   F   158. For me, money is just a means to various ends, and I get no pleasure out of looking at, handling, and feeling it.

My raw score for Greed: _____

Sloth Items (Scale 5)

T   F   159. I would rather learn to accept myself as I am than exert myself to become less sinful.

T   F   160. Often I think something is a good idea, set out to do it, and then lose interest in it before it is finished.

T   F   161. I seldom find that I am so busy doing little things that my important tasks get neglected.

T   F   162. Often I feel just too tired or weak to do much of any-thing.

T   F   163. One thing that helps me avoid thinking about really serious and important problems I can't solve is to keep as busy with other things as I can.

T   F   164. Much of the time I feel hopeless about life.

T F 165. I am seldom bothered by feelings of guilt.

T F 166. Since even the expert theologians disagree, there is no point in my concerning myself about the right way to work out my relationship with God.

T F 167. For me, prayer requires such intense concentration that I never find myself lulled into drowsiness or sleep while praying.

T F 168. God just didn't give me sufficient personal resources to live up to His standards.

T F 169. Sometimes I feel as though nothing in life seems really worth doing.

T F 170. It is foolish to put off dealing with one's personal relationship to God until the many pressing social problems of the day have been solved.

T F 171. Through long experience I have come to the conclusion that it's no use trying to fight sin.

T F 172. When I have a disagreeable task to do I usually tackle it immediately and get it over with rather than put it off until the last minute.

T F 173. I believe that prayer should be effortless and spontaneous rather than something you work at whether you feel like it or not.

T F 174. A good relationship with God is worth all the time and effort one has to spend in devotional exercises.

T F 175. I would rather tackle my work than sit around talking with congenial people.

T F 176. I seldom get to the point where I feel like quitting and must just force myself to keep going.

T F 177. Even though the doctors say I am physically healthy I have a funny kind of laziness and fatigue.

T F 178. I would prefer an easy, comfortable life where I need to exert myself as little as possible to a life full of challenges and demands on my ingenuity and energy.

T F 179. Nearly always I seem to have plenty of energy.

T F 180. I keep myself so busy that I rarely have time to think about God and religion.

T F 181. I am full of enthusiasm about most of the things I do and make the most of my experiences.

T   F   182. Often I feel worthless.

T   F   183. I never get enough comfort or consolation out of religious practices.

T   F   184. No matter how bad things look now, there is always hope for the future.

T   F   185. Much of the time I am angry with myself.

T   F   186. Some things that look like willful acts of sin may be based on psychological weakness and therefore cannot be controlled by the individual.

T   F   187. Very seldom do I feel low-spirited and sad.

T   F   188. A "middle of the road" position with respect to God and religion would never be enough for me.

T   F   189. Since World War II and the concentration camps, man senses his isolation in a way completely unknown to the people of Christ's time.

T   F   190. Most of the projects I undertake I manage to bring to a successful conclusion.

T   F   191. Long ago I came to the conclusion that I don't have the willpower to break most of my bad habits.

T   F   192. Just lying around relaxing for a whole day would be unbearable for me.

T   F   193. Even when I am trying my best to make decisions myself, I somehow find that I drift along and let circumstances settle things for me.

T   F   194. I cannot agree that nearly everything in a human being's life is futile.

T   F   195. When a man is overwhelmed with personal or physical problems, he can't be expected to live up to God's standards.

T   F   196. When I decide I need to change one of my habitual behaviors, I have every confidence that I can do so.

T   F   197. I have often fallen asleep when saying my evening prayers.

T   F   198. I seldom feel sad or depressed because I have to admit to myself that I am not trying very hard to live close to God.

T   F   199. It is a poor idea to postpone prayer and religious exercises until you are in what feels like the right frame of mind to do them effectively.

T   F   200. There are too many books presenting conflicting views about religion for a person to be able to make up their mind on the subject these days.

T   F   201. My conscience often bothers me with the feeling that I am not doing what I ought to be doing.

My raw score for Sloth: _____

Lust Items (Scale 6)

T   F   202. There are many things in life more important than sensuous pleasure.

T   F   203. Sexual enjoyment is God's greatest gift to human beings.

T   F   204. The fact that sexual activity feels so good doesn't make it right.

T   F   205. If I had to choose, I would rather have spiritual closeness with God than physical closeness with other human beings.

T   F   206. My interest in people of the opposite sex is about average, but it certainly doesn't occupy my mind more than anything else.

T   F   207. In the light of current knowledge, the curbs which religion places on human sexual behavior are outmoded and ought to be changed.

T   F   208. I have never found myself somewhat envious of professional therapists whose work often involves hearing about the intimate details of other people's love lives.

T   F   209. No one can tell me when and how and with whom I can make love.

T   F   210. Sigmund Freud did a lot of damage by persuading the world that people should be set free from their sexual inhibitions.

T   F   211. People can get along relatively well without sex if their circumstances and beliefs make it necessary.

T   F   212. Most of the things I do are to avoid trouble rather than to find enjoyment.

T   F   213. If the people who have occupied themselves with ultimate problems like God and life after death had concentrated on the study of human sexual behavior and how to enrich it, the world would be a better place today.

T   F   214. If I have a choice I will go to see a sexy movie in preference to most others.

T   F   215. Society has surrounded people's sex drive with too many prohibitions.

T   F   216. In the final analysis, pleasure is the main thing in life.

T   F   217. I don't especially enjoy watching movies depicting intimate love scenes.

T   F   218. I think that sexual inhibitions are at the root of most people's problems.

T   F   219. God and my beliefs about Him have more control over my behavior than my sexual desires.

T   F   220. If I had a religion which taught that God forbade me every form of sexual pleasure, I would give up my religion.

T   F   221. I think that any religion which teaches that God made man with a sex drive and then set up so many restrictions on it is unreasonable.

T   F   222. I have often found myself wishing I could be a movie actor or actress because so many of them appear to lead virtually free love lives.

T   F   223. Although I believe a healthy sex life is important, it is far less important than many other things in life.

T   F   224. I think I could give up about anything except sexual feelings, thoughts, and pleasures.

T   F   225. I have never spent much time thinking about new and unusual ways to enhance the pleasure of lovemaking.

T   F   226. People who think they don't live for pleasure are just kidding themselves.

T   F   227. To me, it is just as important to give pleasure to a love partner as to get pleasure for myself.

T F 228. It is not difficult to be completely faithful to one's marriage partner.

T F 229. If I have a choice, I pick up and read suggestive magazines rather than magazines on current events.

T F 230. God and religious rules were invented by people to help them control their sexual drives whether they know it or not.

T F 231. For some strange reason, I feel that forbidden sensual pleasures are more exciting and interesting than those which are not forbidden.

T F 232. The kinds of pleasure I think about most are those involving touch and physical contact with other people.

T F 233. Conversations about sex are less interesting to me than conversations about religion.

T F 234. I enjoy parties most when people tell off-color jokes and the conversation is generally suggestive.

T F 235. I would rather read novels which come to grips with man's philosophical and religious problems than those which describe people making love.

T F 236. The notion of a God who is opposed to people enjoying themselves together whenever they have the opportunity is a cruel and inhumane idea.

T F 237. I don't think God would mind if I had an occasional sexual indiscretion.

T F 238. Even during a sexual embrace, I would still place God first rather than set Him and His will aside.

T F 239. I must admit that the teaching expressed in the novel, *Brave New World*, that "everybody belongs to everybody else" sexually is appealing to me.

T F 240. It is nearly impossible to be in the company of an attractive person of the opposite sex without thinking about touching, embracing, kissing, or going to bed with them.

My raw score for Lust: _____

Gluttony Items (Scale 7)

T   F   241. I cannot understand those people who seek out and devour religious experiences almost as if they were starving and such experiences were food.

T   F   242. I really enjoy savoring the fine points of scholarship or the artistry of fine writing in a novel.

T   F   243. My meals are more enjoyable when I can feel free to eat as fast as I wish without worrying about impolitely finishing before others at the table.

T   F   244. One thing I find difficult to understand is how some people can drink ten or twelve cups of coffee throughout the day.

T   F   245. I do not enjoy reading cookbooks or magazine articles on new and interesting ways to prepare food.

T   F   246. I prefer the company of people who drink moderately or not at all.

T   F   247. Frequently I find that I have eaten so much I just don't feel like doing anything but lying around.

T   F   248. Much of the time I have to be concerned about my weight since I tend to be heavier than I should be.

T   F   249. I don't care much about what I have to eat, as long as my meals are balanced and nutritious.

T   F   250. I am not one of those people who get so engrossed in the appreciation of excellent religious art that I forget the religious significance temporarily.

T   F   251. No one has ever told me seriously that I should eat less between meals.

T   F   252. Any religion which taught that people should give as much money to God as they spend on food would be silly.

T   F   253. One reason I do not like to eat and drink too much is that overindulgence dulls my mind and prevents me from pursuing really important things.

T   F   254. I spend more money on alcoholic beverages than I give to God.

T   F   255. Something I especially enjoy is dining at a fine restaurant where I can choose exquisitely prepared gourmet dishes.

T   F   256. I would rather go to a party where plenty of liquor is served than one where people are congenial but very little is offered to drink.

T   F   257. When I want to have a good time I would rather do something active like bowling, swimming, or playing tennis, than sit around drinking with a congenial group of friends.

T   F   258. I seem nearly always to be hungry.

T   F   259. When I go out for a good time I would rather go to a good restaurant for dinner than see a good movie.

T   F   260. I am tired of being told I should cut down on the amount of alcohol I consume.

T   F   261. I would not care to have fine wines served with my evening meals every day.

T   F   262. I get so much pleasure out of the feeling of God's nearness and fellowship that I find myself concentrating on the enjoyment rather than on God and His will.

T   F   263. If I felt that denying myself food for a few days would help me to pray more earnestly and thus gain a deep religious experience, I would gladly do so.

T   F   264. I am quite finicky and particular about what foods I eat.

T   F   265. I think it would be ideal to be in a constant state of ecstasy.

T   F   266. I seldom eat my meals faster than others at the table with me.

T   F   267. I can get so wrapped up in study just because I crave knowledge that I often forget other things, even the people around me.

T   F   268. For me, the intellectual brilliance of the great philosophers is so exciting that religious teachings seem dull by comparison.

T   F   269. I could never get so involved in the pursuit of a hobby that it interfered with my functioning in other important areas of life.

T   F   270. It doesn't matter much to me what I have to eat, as long as I have enough to enable me to live a full life.

T   F   271. It is easy for me to enjoy rich and tasty desserts even after I know I have eaten enough and feel full.

T   F   272. I seldom think of eating between meals.

T   F   273. It is difficult for me to understand why so many people stuff themselves at meals.

T   F   274. When listening to great religious music, I am much more aware of and responsive to the message communicated than to the power of the music to move me emotionally.

T   F   275. One of the things I would most like to do if I had plenty of money is keep a well-stocked liquor cabinet.

T   F   276. I often find myself reluctant to leave the state of peace one finds in church or at prayer and return to the turmoil of the world.

T   F   277. My willpower is weak when it comes to passing up food or drink.

T   F   278. My philosophy of life is pretty well summed up by the phrase, "Eat, drink and be merry, for tomorrow we die."

T   F   279. I am sometimes so busy I can't get around to eating some of my meals.

T   F   280. One of my weaknesses is a liking for rich or sweet snacks between meals.

My raw score for Gluttony: _____

Scoring the Sin Test

Be sure that you complete the Sin Test before you do the following. When you have answered *all* 280 items with either *T* or *F*, proceed to score your answers. Carefully follow these directions for scoring:

1. Use the scoring key on page 238 to mark each item you answered in the "sinful" direction. Those are the items NOT in agreement with the scoring key. Score all seven scales.
2. Count the number of "sinful" responses you gave to the Pride Scale items and write that number in the space provided at the end of the Pride Scale. Follow the same procedure with the Envy Scale and the other scales, writing the number of "sinful" responses at the end of each scale.
3. Enter the total sin scores for each of the seven scales below. These are the raw scores for the various scales.
4. You will next transform these raw scores into *scaled* scores. You can use the *Conversion Table* on page 239 to find the equivalent scaled score for each raw score. Then enter the scaled scores on page 240.

Finding the scaled scores will let you know something about what your results mean. After you have determined the scaled score for each sin, you will be able to meaningfully compare your sin scores with one another. Moreover, your scaled score can be used to determine how your scores compare with those of a norm group of professional church workers. *Scaled* scores can be understood as follows: 50=average—one half the norm group scored higher and one half scored lower; 40=below average—only 15.86% of the norm group scored lower; 30=so far below average (less sinful) that only 2.27% of the norm group scored lower; 60=above average—only 15.86% of the norm group scored higher; 70=so far above average (more sinful) that only 2.27% of the norm group scored higher.

Record your Raw Scores:

Pride	_____	**Sloth**	_____
Envy	_____	**Lust**	_____
Anger	_____	**Gluttony**	_____
Greed	_____		

Raw Scoring Key

1. T	41. F	81. F	121. F	161. F	201. F	241. T
2. F	42. F	82. F	122. F	162. F	202. T	242. F
3. F	43. F	83. T	123. T	163. F	203. F	243. F
4. T	44. F	84. T	124. F	164. F	204. T	244. T
5. F	45. T	85. T	125. T	165. T	205. T	245. T
6. F	46. T	86. F	126. T	166. F	206. T	246. T
7. T	47. F	87. T	127. F	167. F	207. F	247. F
8. F	48. T	88. T	128. F	168. F	208. F	248. F
9. T	49. T	89. F	129. F	169. F	209. F	249. T
10. T	50. T	90. F	130. T	170. T	210. T	250. T
11. F	51. F	91. T	131. F	171. F	211. T	251. T
12. F	52. T	92. F	132. F	172. T	212. T	252. F
13. F	53. F	93. F	133. F	173. F	213. F	253. T
14. F	54. F	94. T	134. F	174. T	214. F	254. F
15. T	55. F	95. F	135. T	175. T	215. F	255. F
16. T	56. F	96. F	136. F	176. F	216. F	256. F
17. F	57. T	97. T	137. F	177. F	217. T	257. T
18. F	58. F	98. F	138. F	178. F	218. F	258. F
19. F	59. F	99. T	139. F	179. T	219. T	259. F
20. F	60. F	100. F	140. T	180. F	220. F	260. F
21. F	61. T	101. T	141. T	181. T	221. F	261. T
22. F	62. F	102. T	142. F	182. F	222. F	262. F
23. F	63. F	103. F	143. F	183. F	223. T	263. T
24. T	64. T	104. T	144. F	184. T	224. F	264. F
25. T	65. F	105. F	145. T	185. F	225. T	265. F
26. F	66. F	106. F	146. F	186. F	226. F	266. F
27. T	67. T	107. F	147. F	187. T	227. T	267. F
28. T	68. T	108. F	148. T	188. T	228. T	268. F
29. T	69. F	109. F	149. F	189. F	229. F	269. T
30. F	70. F	110. F	150. F	190. T	230. F	270. T
31. T	71. F	111. T	151. T	191. F	231. F	271. F
32. T	72. T	112. F	152. T	192. T	232. F	272. T
33. T	73. F	113. F	153. T	193. F	233. T	273. T
34. F	74. T	114. F	154. F	194. F	234. F	274. T
35. F	75. F	115. F	155. T	195. F	235. T	275. F
36. F	76. T	116. T	156. T	196. T	236. F	276. F
37. F	77. F	117. F	157. F	197. F	237. F	277. F
38. F	78. F	118. T	158. T	198. T	238. T	278. F
39. T	79. F	119. T	159. F	199. T	239. F	279. T
40. F	80. T	120. F	160. F	200. F	240. F	280. F

Conversion Table: Raw Scores to Scaled Scores

Raw Score	Pride	Envy	Anger	Greed	Sloth	Lust	Gluttony
1		31	—	—	—	33	—
2	26	33	31	20	—	36	—
3	29	35	33	23	—	38	—
4	31	38	36	26	27	40	28
5	34	40	38	28	29	42	30
6	36	42	41	31	31	44	32
7	38	44	43	33	33	46	35
8	41	47	45	36	35	48	37
9	43	49	48	39	37	50	39
10	46	51	50	41	38	52	41
11	48	53	53	44	40	55	44
12	51	56	55	46	42	57	46
13	53	58	57	49	44	59	48
14	56	60	60	51	46	61	50
15	58	63	62	54	48	63	52
16	60	65	65	57	49	65	55
17	63	67	67	59	51	67	57
18	65	69	69	62	53	69	59
19	68	72	72	64	55	71	61
20	70	74	74	67	57	74	63
21	73	76	77	70	59	75	66
22	75	78	79	72	60	78	68
23	77	81	81	75	62	80	70
24	80	83	84	77	64	82	72
25	82	84	86	80	66	84	74
26	85	86	87	83	68	86	77
27	87	88	92	85	70	88	79
28		90	94	88	71	91	81
29		92	97	90	73	93	83
30			99	91	75	95	85
31				92	77	97	87
32				95	78	98	89
33				97	80	99	
34				99	82	101	
35					84	103	
36					86	105	
37					88	107	
38					90		
39					91		
40					93		

Record your Scaled Scores derived from the table:

Pride   _____

Envy   _____

Anger   _____

Greed   _____

Sloth   _____

Lust   _____

Gluttony   _____

What Your Scaled Scores Mean

The Sin Test results may be useful as thought starters. This test may be helpful, but it should not be taken as a precise measure of your sins. Only God knows our hearts, and we cannot yet know as we are fully known by Him (1 Corinthians 13:12).

These *scaled* scores can be compared with one another (raw scores cannot be compared). By referring to scaled scores, you can see which of the Seven Deadly Sins is/are most troublesome in your life and/or for others with whom you are living or working. And you can note your lowest scores. These scores suggest which sins are probably least troublesome for you and others who know you.

You can also determine how your scores compare with those of the norm group (a group of about a hundred people who dedicate their lives to Christian work). Although such persons, because they are human, are sinful, too, we might expect their scores to be normal rather than exceptionally high or exceptionally low. The scaled score has been designed to contrast your results with this group of people.

Scaled scores below 40 may suggest an extremely high level of goodness. They might, however, accompany a tendency to see oneself in an unrealistically good light. Prayer for full self-knowledge and deeper self-understanding may be suggested by such low scores.

Scaled scores between 40 and 54 are in the average range. Most Christians will score in this range.

Scaled scores between 55 and 64 are above average, suggesting a need for self-examination in the light of daily Scripture study.

Scaled scores between 65 and 74 are high, suggesting a need for thorough self-examination in the light of daily Scripture study and perhaps counseling with a pastor, a spiritual director, or a spiritual counselor.

Scaled scores of 75 and above are very high; they may result from a tendency to suffer from unrealistic guilt, such as occurs in some depressed persons, and so might be elevated due to lack of objectivity caused by a mood disorder. A consultation with a pastor, spiritual director, or spiritual counselor may be helpful.

Appendix 2

The Sin Test and Psychopathology

In order to test the idea that sin and what we now call "emotional illness" might be closely related, I developed the Sin Test and administered it experimentally to volunteers.

The Sin Test consists of seven scales, one for each of the Seven Deadly Sins, containing approximately forty True/False items each. Items were constructed from descriptions of the Seven Deadly Sins found in the writings of various Christian moral theologians. After administering the Sin Test to several different groups (explained and defined earlier in this book), significant relationships between the sins and psychopathology were found.* A brief account of selected relationships follows.

The Sin Test and MMPI Scale Correlations

All of these correlations were positive and statistically significant. Readers not familiar with MMPI interpretation should not assume that the names of the scales (though reported here)

---

*These volunteers also completed the Minnesota Multiphasic Personality Inventory (*MMPI*), and charts containing psychiatric diagnoses and descriptions were available for the inpatient group.

are interchangeable with diagnoses. MMPI scales are descriptive, but diagnostic impressions are based on the total profile configuration, not on individual scales. Here are some of the relationships that were found between the Sin Test scales and MMPI scales:

- Pride was correlated with MMPI Scale 2 (Depression), MMPI Scale 6 (Paranoia), and MMPI Scale 8 (Schizophrenia).
- Envy was correlated with MMPI Scale 2 (Depression), MMPI Scale 7 (Psychasthenia), and MMPI Scale 8 (Schizophrenia).
- Anger was correlated with MMPI Scale 7 (Psychasthenia), and MMPI Scale 8 (Schizophrenia).
- Greed had no correlative scales that were testable within the limits of the experimental data.
- Sloth was correlated with MMPI Scale 2 (Depression), MMPI Scale 4 (Psychopathic Deviate), MMPI Scale 7 (Psychasthenia), MMPI Scale 8 (Schizophrenia), and MMPI Scale 9 (Hypomania).
- Lust was correlated with MMPI Scale 4 (Psychopathic Deviate), MMPI Scale 8 (Schizophrenia), and MMPI Scale 9 (Hypomania).
- Gluttony was correlated with MMPI Scale 7 (Psychasthenia) and MMPI Scale 9 (Hypomania).
- All the Sin Scales except Lust and Gluttony were correlated with MMPI Scale 0 (Social Introversion).

The Sin Test and Psychiatric Diagnosis

The inpatients who volunteered to take the Sin Test had hospital charts with psychiatric diagnoses. Relationships between the Sin Scales and diagnoses and/or descriptions from the charts of these patients demonstrated that the Sin Scales are positively related to psychopathology. For one thing, there is a consistent trend toward higher total Sin Test scores for psychiatric patients than for nonpatients. Moreover, certain Sin Scales were significantly related to specific diagnoses. Three diagnostic groups among the available inpatients were considered large enough to yield meaningful data. Positive and significant relationships were found between specific diagnostic groups and specific Sin Scales:

- Sloth scores were significantly higher (and Pride, Greed, and Lust scores were lower) for patients with a diagnosis of depression.
- Pride scores were significantly higher for patients with schizophrenic diagnoses. Also notably higher for this group were Anger and Greed.
- The mean Sin Scale scores for schizophrenics were higher on all the Sin Scales than were those of other inpatients. The question of the relationship between thought disorder and sin was raised by this phenomenon. When all patients given any psychotic diagnosis (including brain syndromes) were grouped together, their scores on the Pride scale were significantly higher than those of patients without a thought disorder diagnosis.

A Caution About Use of These Findings

For readers unaccustomed to working with means and statistical significance, an emphatic note of caution: The Sin Scales *cannot be used to diagnose mental illness.* Serious and damaging results could occur from any attempt to equate Sin Scale scores with psychopathology. The correlations reported are *relationships*, not *identities*. Simplified, this means that if a positive relationship is known to exist between Sin Scale #1 and psychiatric diagnosis #2, given a large group of people with high scores on Sin Scale #1, *some members of this group, a number greater than would occur by chance,* might be given the psychiatric diagnosis predicted by the relationship. *Some, but not all.* Example: If you take the Sin Test and have a high score on the Sloth Scale, this does not necessarily mean that a psychologist would find that you are depressed. But if a hundred people have high scores on the Sloth Scale, a large number of them likely will be found to be depressed.

What Do My Scores Mean?

The most useful results for you might be better self-understanding and a helpful grasp of which sins are most problematic for you. Your findings may answer the question, "What should I be praying about and working to overcome?" But more than that, your scores can guide you to reread the discussions of your more troublesome sin traits and how to battle against them.

Raw Scores and T-Scores

If you wish to be able to compare your Sin Test scores with one another, and with the scores of the norm group, you cannot use the total number of scorable items for each scale. Those scores are called raw scores. To make them comparable, you must transform them into T-scores (scaled scores).

Appendix 3

More History of the Seven Deadly Sins

The origin of the list known as the Seven Deadly Sins remains uncertain. At least as old as institutional Christianity, the scheme may be even more venerable. What is certain, according to Morton Bloomfield, is that the list came out of the Hellenistic world, a culture synthesized from elements of West and East, old and new.[1]

The astrological theory traces the sins to the gnostic notion of a "Soul Journey." The soul, pure because of its nonmaterial substance, descends from God through the seven spheres of the planets. At the portal for each sphere it receives one of the traits of corporeal existence, evil because of its material quality. The list of the sins, Bloomfield holds, had its origin from this blend of Hebrew and Zoroastrian thinking. One problem encountered by proponents of the astrological hypothesis is that the earliest Christian list, that of Evagrius, includes eight, not seven, deadly sins.[2]

Others trace the origin of the sins to the great pre-Christian writers of Stoicism. Horace, in a letter, lists seven: *avaritia* (avarice), *laudis amor* (love of praise), *invidia* (envy), *iracundia* (wrath), *inertia* (idleness), *vinositas* (drunkenness), and *amor* (lust).[3]

Modern attempts to combine elements existing in such earlier writings into a scheme that could be thought of as a predecessor of the earliest Christian list have invariably led to a great deal of juggling of terms and to numerous tours de force, which weaken the argument considerably.[4]

Siegfried Wenzel has argued for the specifically Christian origin of the list, noting that all the sins appear in the New Testament, that their names all occur in Origen's writings, and that Jesus spoke once of seven spirits replacing the one demon originally drawn out of a man (Matthew 12:43–45). According to this argument, the first Christian list of the sins came from Origen and the Bible.

In spite of the inconclusive results of speculation about earliest sources, it is generally agreed that the structure in its Christian form was developed by ascetics in the Egyptian desert where it was in common use by the time Evagrius of Pontus wrote down the earliest Christian list known.[5] Eight sins were included: gluttony, vainglory, fornication, pride, wrath, sorrow, indifference, and avarice.[6]

Brought to the West from the lore of the Egyptian hermits by John Cassian, the Seven Deadly Sins concept was incorporated into his two treatises for the monasteries founded by him at Marseille (*De Institutis Coenobiorum* [c. A.D. 420] and *Collationes Patrum* [c. A.D. 425–428]). Cassian's description of *acidie* (or sloth) in the *Institutes* has been cited earlier in this book because it furnishes a striking demonstration of the clinical style already in use at that early time for describing the sins.

Cassian's list, identical with Evagrius's, was of value primarily to monastics. The scheme spread to the monasteries of the Celtic Church and there through the introduction of confession for the laity became a device used for the examination of lay penitents. Thus, the notion of cardinal sins became familiar in Western Christendom.

A century and a half after Cassian, Pope Gregory the Great lent the weight of papal authority to the framework, but not without altering the list in important ways. In his *Moralia*, Gregory shortened the catalog to seven vices rather than eight. *Superbia* (pride) was, for Gregory, the underlying vice from which all the others flowed; consequently he removed it from the list, along with *acedia* (indifference). His single addition was *invidia* (envy). Gregory placed *vana gloria* (vainglory) at the head of his list, and moved *gula* (gluttony) and *luxuria* (lust) to the end.[7]

For centuries the two structures (Cassian's and Gregory's) existed side by side with various writers identifying *acedia* with *tristitia* (sorrow), (e.g., Theodulf of Orleans [c. eighth century] writes of "*acedia sive tristitia*"; both Hugh of St. Victor and Peter Lombard in the twelfth century used the expression, "*acedia vel tristitia*"). Peter Lombard's influential *Sententiae* assured for *acedia* a permanent place in the list so that it became the standard term, instead of *tristitia*, for the sin now known as "sloth."[8] Usage also restored *superbia* to the list in place of *vana gloria*.

Thus a somewhat modified Gregorian catalog of the sins gradually became dominant: *superbia, ira, invidia, avaritia, acedia, gula,* and *luxuria*.[9] It was in this form that the sin list came to Dante, Chaucer, Gower, and the countless other writers, artists, and preachers who described the sins. In this form they found their way into confessors' manuals from the twelfth century on as a handy list for examination of penitents.

There are numerous references to the sin list in literature. One of the earliest is *The Parson's Tale* in Chaucer's *Canterbury Tales*. Langland's *Piers Plowman* deals with the Seven, as do Spenser's *The Faerie Queene* and Marlowe's *Doctor Faustus*. Milton and Dante scatter references to the Seven individually through their works.

Among all the artists who depicted the sins in their work, the Dutch painter Hieronymous Bosch (1450–1516) stands out. Bosch painted a tabletop depicting the Seven Deadly Sins in a detail of *The Eye of God which Sees the Committing of the Seven Deadly Sins* (oil on panel, Museo del Prado, Madrid).

The long history of the Seven Deadly Sins, their tenacity and unquenchable vitality as behavior descriptions, and the apparent near-universality of the fascination they have held as concepts, all suggest that the framework contains relevant truths about human behavior and its organization.

Notes

1. Morton W. Bloomfield, *The Seven Deadly Sins* (East Lansing: Michigan State College Press, 1952), n.p.
2. Siegfried Wenzel, *The Sin of Sloth: "Acedia" in Medieval Thought and Literature* (Chapel Hill, N.C.: University of North Carolina Press, 1967), n.p.
3. Ludwig Ruland, *Foundations of Morality*, trans. T. A. Rattler, ed. Thomas Newton (St. Louis: B. Herder, 1930), 105–106.
4. Op. cit., 15–16.
5. Ibid.
6. Bloomfield, 44.
7. Ibid., 72.
8. Wenzel, 29.
9. Op. cit., 72–73.